DOS VSAM
for Application
Programmers

to my parents

DOS VSAM
for Application Programmers

Lana J. Chandler

 TAB Professional and Reference Books

Division of TAB BOOKS Inc.
Blue Ridge Summit, PA

A Petrocelli book

FIRST EDITION
FIRST PRINTING

Copyright © 1989 by TAB BOOKS Inc.
Printed in the United States of America

Library of Congress Cataloging in Publication Data

Chandler, Lana J.
    DOS VSAM for application programmers / by Lana J. Chandler.
        p.   cm.
    Bibliography: p.
    Includes index.
    ISBN 0-8306-3251-4 (pbk.)
    1. Virtual storage (Computer science)   2. Operating systems
(Computers)   I. Title.
QA76.9.V5C42   1989
005.4'3—dc19   89-4254
                                                              CIP

TAB BOOKS Inc. offers software for sale. For information and a
catalog, please contact TAB Software Department, Blue Ridge
Summit, PA 17294-0850.

Questions regarding the content of this book should be addressed to:

    Reader Inquiry Branch
    TAB BOOKS Inc.
    Blue Ridge Summit, PA 17294-0214

Edited by Roman H. Gorski

Contents

Introduction

As programmers, we are masters of many skills. Being a good coder isn't enough in today's high-tech environment. Our profession demands that we acquire a great deal more than a working knowledge of languages like COBOL or BASIC. We must be able to read and write JCL in order to connect our programs with the correct physical devices and files.

Who hasn't gotten a dump? If you want to survive in this profession, debugging skills are a "must."

Communication skills are necessary. Programmers work with users to design and implement software enhancements. You might even be called upon to write supporting documentation for users, operators and other programmers.

Should you write a program without employing any planning skills? No. Both development and maintenance require up-front planning. First, we discover what is needed, then we map our approach by using such tools as templates and flowcharting symbols.

It helps to know how libraries are structured. Understanding core image, source statement, relocatable and procedure libraries can be a real plus when trying to develop and execute programs.

Understanding when and how to use utilities such as SORT and DITTO is important. These flexible and easy-to-use programs are great at helping you streamline certain tasks.

The list of needed skills is practically endless. The point is that a programmer's education must never be limited to language. That's why I wrote this book, because VSAM is one of those "extra skills" most application programmers need.

The term *VSAM* is an acronym for "virtual storage access method." Why do you, as a programmer, need to be concerned about this particular access method? The reason is—it's popular! VSAM is great, especially for random processing. It provides you with more flexibility in file handling logic.

Generally viewed as ISAM's replacement, VSAM was introduced in the mid-1970s. It is a device-independent method; simply, that means it works the same regardless of the DASD model. Interestingly enough, though, only in the last couple of years have we seen a significant number of files migrating towards VSAM processing.

Did you notice that I used the term *migrate*?

Actually, that's a pretty accurate description of how many data centers introduce VSAM processing. Some DASD models, such as the 3350s, will not support ISAM files. The latter must be converted to native VSAM files, or ISAM Interface Programs (commonly referred to as IIPs) must be used. By using an IIP to simulate VSAM processing, your data center can, in a sense, "migrate" to VSAM. I'll show you how the IIP can be your first step toward converting ISAM systems to VSAM.

Unlike ISAM, native VSAM offers multiple organizational structures. I'll show you the similarities and differences among key-sequenced, entry-sequenced, and relative-record files.

I'll illustrate the impact VSAM has on DOS JCL. Sample job streams have been included to clarify coding requirements.

Unlike other access methods, VSAM needs the support of a utility program. Frankly, you can't really be successful at using VSAM without understanding some of the basic components of the Access Method Services (AMS) program. AMS includes numerous control statements (enough to fill an entire book!). I've included some of the more popular commands and options, along with sample output.

Tuning is important when dealing with VSAM files, especially if the file experiences growth activity. Getting the best performance possible demands regular monitoring and knowing what to look for.

Should access to a file be limited to certain people? VSAM was designed to include password protection features.

Tips on how to best ensure recovery of a file have been included. Both catalog and file recovery procedures need to be considered when VSAM files are involved.

Recognize the need for standards when implementing VSAM in your data center. Establish guidelines to help achieve consistency, such as in the case of user vs. master catalogs. File names are another important area where standardization pays off.

Are you weary of running out of space for SAM files and then having to recode EXTENT statements? Perhaps VSAM Space Management for SAM files is worth your consideration. I'll highlight how this particular feature of the VSAM package can be used as a disk management system for SAM files.

I hope that this guide leaves you with a better understanding of what VSAM can do. It's important that you, as a programmer, stay technically current, and learning more about VSAM is definitely a step in the right direction.

VSAM not only influences programmer code, but if you also consider AMS control statements, it's practically the same as learning another language. I want to help you get better acquainted with VSAM's multidimensional personality.

Expand your creative talents! Let me show you how flexible and powerful VSAM can be.

1

What Is VSAM?

All files are not created equal.

When it comes to DASD files and how they may be accessed by programs, IBM certainly adopted the philosophy of "different strokes for different folks." Recognizing the need for data to be organized and retrieved in different ways, we identify file structures by what are commonly referred to as *access methods*.

Before I explain the basic types of access methods, let's look at data hierarchy.

Most of the information used by your programs is stored on DASD. DASD is an acronym for "direct access storage device." This particular piece of hardware is the most popular storage medium. Requiring little operator intervention to create or retire them, DASD files offer programmers a great deal of flexibility. Files housed on DASD can be organized in such a way that they are read sequentially or directly (randomly) by a specific key, such as an item number in the case of an inventory system.

Did you notice the term *key*? Like the key to your house, a file's key is unique. It provides a way to quickly access a specific record, just like your house key opens a specific door.

Keys consist of one or more fields. When designing a file, the key fields must be so noted. Furthermore, the programming languages you use have certain conventions for defining and referencing key fields.

Fields make up keys.
Fields make up records.
Records make up files.
Must every file have a key?

No. However, as we'll shortly discover, some access methods do demand keys.

A *record* is a collection of data sharing a common purpose. For example, an Inventory File usually contains a record for each item kept in inventory. One record might contain information related to letter-size file folders, while another record is used to house the same type of data on 12-inch rulers. Along with the item number, examples of fields comprising each item's record may be the number of items in stock, the vendor, and the date last ordered.

As already stated, each item more than likely will require an individual record. Together, these records make up an Inventory File. A file is an organized collection of related information. Our Inventory File, therefore, contains information related to all the supply items stocked by a company.

It's difficult to be in data processing today and not have come across the term *on-line*. On-line processing refers to the operation of input/output devices under direct control of the CPU (central processing unit). [CRTs (cathode ray tubes) are used to communicate with the computer.] To the user, on-line means almost instantaneous response to requests. Such requests may vary in nature depending on the application involved. In a brokerage house, money may be deducted from a customer's account when a buy order is given to stocks. In a library, a student might request a search of all book titles by a specific author.

Returning to our inventory example, on-line processing can be used to immediately reduce the stock on hand when supplies are distributed. Through query screens, a person can use a CRT to inquire about the available quantity. Perhaps supplies are distributed by 10 individuals. With each distribution, quantity is reduced, thus providing all 10 people with an awareness of what is going on. If there are 50 boxes of letter-size file folders in stock and 5 people have each distributed 10 boxes, an inquiry will show there are no more boxes available for distribution regardless of which of the 10 people attempts to fill the next order.

Through access methods, file structures and programming logic, we can build DASD files that support on-line activities. In the case of our Inventory System and the letter-size file folders, an item number would be required by the CRT operator to reference any information related to the folders. By using an access method that supports key fields, a specific record can be quickly located without a sequential reading of all records on the file.

Are keys reserved for just on-line processing?

No. Batch applications may also benefit from file structures which allow keys. Whereas on-line processing involves the complete handling of an individual transaction as soon as someone enters it, batch processing involves accumulating transactions and then posting them all in the same run. People don't sit down at CRTs and enter transactions which immediately impact batch files. After data entry people key in all the transactions through CRTs, 5280s, keypunch machines, etc., a computer operator instructs the machine to run specific jobs that edit, post and report such transactional activities. Again, going back to our inventory example, in a batch environment, those 10 people distributing supplies would be unaware that the stock was exhausted until the batch run was made or promised supplies couldn't be found for an irate customer!

It can take a long time to read a large file. Perhaps only 10 percent of the file is actually updated each time the application is processed. Why bother to waste time and resources reading the other 90 percent of the file? Using keys, programs can be designed to access only that needed 10 percent.

The data management programs that come with DOS (disk operating system) provide a variety of methods for gaining access to files. These methods are designed around file organization and data access techniques. Even the model of DASD used by your data center can influence access methods.

For example, newer models of DASD will not support ISAM files; such files must be converted to native VSAM, or an IIP (ISAM Interface Program) must be used.

So that we don't get ahead of ourselves, however, let's highlight the basic access methods supported by DOS.

1) SAM—Sequential Access Method.

SAM is the only access method available for certain types of input/output devices. Examples of the latter are card punches, card readers, printers, and magnetic tapes. DASD files may be organized as SAM files but don't have to be.

As the name implies, SAM files subscribe to a sequential way of storing data. Records are not organized by key fields nor can they be accessed by keys. One record physically follows another. To access the one-hundredth record on a file, your program must read each of the 99 records which come before it.

When magnetic tape or DASD files are involved, it's usually necessary to eventually add or delete records. When this activity occurs on a SAM file, the file must be physically written out as a new file. That's why we have input and output files in programs which add or delete records to SAM files.

Since SAM does not provide a means to directly access a specific record, it's easy to see why this particular access method doesn't lend itself to on-line processing. Imagine how poor response time would be if a dozen people queried a file consisting of 50,000 records and the computer read each record individually!

2) DAM—Direct Access Method.

The Direct Access Method is limited to DASD files.

DAM files are organized according to a predictable relationship between the key of a record and the physical address of that record. You, the programmer, determine this relationship. Algorithms are often used by programmers to establish the logical and physical relationship of a DAM record.

The physical DASD space allocated to this type of file is available in its entirety for data records; no physical space is required for indexes (that's another way we often refer to keys).

Records are directly stored and retrieved through addresses specified in programs.

When are DAM files generally used?

Typically, this file structure is used when the time required to locate individual records must be kept to an absolute minimum.

3) ISAM—Indexed Sequential Access Method.

In accordance with its name, the Indexed Sequential Access Method is based on an indexing system. Like DAM files, ISAM files are also available only for DASD processing.

ISAM records are physically arranged in a sequence based on a key which is part of every record. This key can consist of one or more fields.

An ISAM file physically consists of three components, and DASD space must be allocated to each component. We have the *prime data area* which houses the records. The *index area* contains the key fields along with a reference to where the related record is physically stored. The *overflow area* holds any new additions (records) since the file was last reorganized.

Because of the indexes, ISAM files may be accessed directly. Remember how we said that when a SAM file is involved, 99 records have to be read before the one-hundredth one can be accessed? If the same file is organized under ISAM, the one-hundredth record can be directly accessed by supplying the appropriate key.

Along with providing rapid access to individual records, ISAM files may also be referenced sequentially.

4) VSAM—Virtual Storage Access Method.

Now we introduce the main topic of our book!

VSAM is more than an access method. When you consider all the "bells and whistles" that come with VSAM (such as the Access Methods Services Program or the ISAM Interface Program), it's enough to fill several texts.

As its name implies, VSAM was designed for virtual storage operating systems. The program that makes up this particular access method resides in virtual storage along with the programs that use it.

For over 10 years, IBM's ISAM was the most popular indexed file handling method in the data processing industry. However, users found some aspects of ISAM to be inefficient and clumsy. One example of a problem area is the addition of new records to an ISAM file. New records are stored in the overflow area until the file is reorganized, thus lengthening access time when one of these records is needed.

To better meet user demands, IBM developed VSAM. First introduced in the mid-1970s, VSAM was supposed to simplify file handling on IBM systems both in terms of JCL and coding logic.

Device independence is achieved. VSAM references a data record by its relative displacement, in bytes, from the beginning of the file rather than by its physical device address. Through the usage of passwords, improved data security is afforded. Also, it is easier to develop JCL for programs referencing VSAM files than if ISAM files are used.

These are some reasons why VSAM is promoted as a more desirable and flexible access method than ISAM. Are we also saying that it's easier to use? No. Like most things in life, you get what you pay for.

VSAM offers a maximum of possibilities for the direct and sequential processing of fixed and variable-length records on DASD, but it's also an amazingly complex access method. Improper usage of VSAM can cost you dearly in system resources. In other words, you can't fake it. If you don't know what you're doing, you'll pay in poor machine performance.

•

Now that we've introduced the most popular access methods for DOS environments, let's take a more in-depth look at how VSAM files may be organized. We'll also spend some time discussing the positive and negative features of DOS VSAM.

First of all, VSAM really offers three different file organizations. Records may be organized in a logical sequence by a key field, in the physical sequence in which they are written into the file or according to the relative record numbers in the file. Through programming logic, records may be added, deleted and modified to all three file types. These file organizational types are called:

1) KSDS—key-sequenced data set
2) ESDS—entry-sequenced data set
3) RRDS—relative-record data set

Throughout this book, the term *data set* is synonymous with *file*.

Let's take a look at the differences and similarities attributed to each file type. In addition, individual chapters have been devoted to each.

KSDS

In key-sequenced data sets, records are organized in a logical manner by keys. Key fields are defined in the programs referencing these files as well as the appropriate AMS utilities (more about the latter in Chapters 6 and 7).

The key fields serve as an index for a KSDS and appear in the same physical position of each record in the file. A unique value must be contained in each key. For example, in an inventory system, the item number may be the key, with each item having a unique number.

VSAM uses keys to build an index. The index in this book connects keywords with the appropriate page numbers. More details about a specific keyword can be found on the page(s) noted in the index. Similarly, a file's index connects a key and the appropriate record. The entire record can be directly accessed through information contained in the index. Records can be retrieved sequentially or directly, depending on how a program is coded. When new records are added to a KSDS, they are loaded into the data set in key sequence.

KSDS VSAM files can generally be processed faster than ISAM files because VSAM was designed with a more efficient indexing feature.

To better explain this statement requires some explanation as to how VSAM files are physically organized on DASD. Later in this chapter, we will review how records are accessed and stored. For the present discussion, however, it's best to limit ourselves to a minimum of terms since our goal is mainly to familiarize you with the three organizational structures available under VSAM.

When new records are added to a KSDS, a physical area called *distributed free space* is used. When such a file is created, certain portions can be left empty. In other words, free DASD space can be distributed throughout the file. Is it only within the initial file that free space can be defined? No. Through changes to the appropriate AMS utilities (more about this in later chapters), the distributed free space allocation may be modified to best suit your needs. In fact, when dealing with a constantly changing file in the sense of additions and deletions, it's important that you keep an eye on this particular aspect of a KSDS.

Records in a KSDS are physically organized by key fields. When a record is added or when an existing one is lengthened, the free space at or near the existing records closest in key sequence is used. Remember how ISAM requires an overflow area? The distributed free space in a KSDS file (which is actually VSAM's equivalent of an indexed file) eliminates the need for an overflow area. In addition, data movement is reduced.

When a record is deleted or shortened, the related DASD area becomes part of the distributed free space. Therefore, you can say that VSAM reclaims space since this area can then be used for new or lengthened records. One real plus to this feature is that the space is reclaimed without anyone having to reorganize the file.

When IBM designed VSAM, it was afforded with a more efficient indexing system than ISAM's. A KSDS index usually requires less DASD space and less updating of index entries. Physical space is minimized by a key compression feature and by blocking index records. VSAM's key compression feature minimizes the space required to store keys. Because of this optimization feature, a key that is defined in a program as being 15 bytes long may be reduced to 3 or 4 bytes internally.

The shorter the index, the less time is required to search and update it. Furthermore, updating is infrequent because the distributed free space reduces the frequency of modifying the indexes when records are added. For example, when a record is added to an ISAM file and the latter is subsequently reorganized, most of the indexes may be changed if it's inserted near the beginning of the file. On the other hand, in a VSAM environment, free space should exist throughout the file, eliminating the need for a shifting of numerous physical locations.

ESDS

Organization within an entry-sequenced data set is dependent on a physical order rather than a logical scheme. There are no key fields defined in an ESDS; no indexes exist.

In accordance with its name, this type of VSAM file is sequenced by the entry in which records appear. The contents of records do not in any way affect where they are physically placed in the file.

When new records are added, they must immediately follow the last existing record on file. Note the word *immediately*. The concept of distributed free space does not exist in regard to an ESDS; that's why new records are placed at the end of the file. Therefore, however you choose to build this type of file is how it will physically exist. Furthermore, records cannot be shortened, deleted or lengthened. They are fixed in length and are physically constant in location to other records on file.

How useful can a file be that doesn't allow for deletions? To use an old saying, "There's more than one way to skin a cat."

One way to provide for deletions is to program the capability yourself. When designing record layouts for an ESDS, include a status field. Through program logic, different values may be moved into such a field. A value of "0" may indicate an active record, while a value of "1" may signify that the record is to be deleted. It's easy to write a program to read the ESDS and to write out a new version of it, omitting those records set to delete status. Such a program includes file definitions for both input and output files. In other words, treat it like a SAM file; the file must be physically written anew each time you want to delete records.

The one point I want to emphasize is that a delete status field is something *you* have to design and code. It is not a feature automatically available under VSAM.

Does an ESDS offer any flexibility in regard to how it can be accessed?

Yes. An ESDS can be accessed sequentially and directly. However, since there is no index associated with an ESDS, the programmer must keep track of a record's relative byte address (RBA) in order to access it directly. The structure of an ESDS lends itself the easiest to sequential access.

RRDS

A relative-record data set contains only fixed-length records. When you build an RRDS, each of its records can be identified with a number that indicates the record's position in the file. Such records are often described as being located in fixed-length *slots*. Each record occupies a slot, and each record is accessed by the slot number which is referred to as the relative-record number.

Regardless of whether a slot is empty or contains data, it is assigned a relative-record number. These numbers range from 1 through the highest number of records that can be physically stored in the file.

When dealing with an RRDS, records may be accessed sequentially or directly.

In the sequential mode, records are accessed in sequentially ascending order by relative-record number. For example, if the file holds 255 records, the first read will start at slot number 1 and progress to slot number 255 with subsequent reads.

Direct access is controlled through program logic. By referencing relative-record numbers, specific records may be accessed.

•

Depending on the file structure selected, VSAM allows for the retrieval, storage, update and deletion of records. Fixed-length as well as variable-length records can be processed.

Access may be direct or sequential. In Appendix B, I've summarized for your convenience the main characteristics of each file type.

Each structure has its own limitations and advantages. When designing a system, you must determine which best suits your needs. The most popular structure for a VSAM file is KSDS. The latter also most closely resembles an ISAM file.

As we continue through this book, you'll discover that the KSDS, ESDS and RRDS structures share many similarities. The primary way they differ is the sequence in which records are stored in them.

DATA ORGANIZATION

To really understand VSAM and how to achieve the best performance possible, you must know the basics of how a VSAM file is physically organized.

A VSAM data set (or file) is also referred to as a *cluster*. When we use this term, we're talking about more than the records which make up the file. (The latter are also referred to as the cluster's *data component*.) In addition to data records, a cluster contains any control areas or indexes associated with the data component. For example, in the case of a KSDS, the cluster refers to both records and indexes.

AMS utilities allow us to designate the physical placement of clusters on DASD. The area on DASD housing a cluster is called a *data space*. All of one cluster, part of one cluster or several clusters may be stored in one data space. An entire DASD volume does not have to be isolated for VSAM data space; the area not defined as data space may be used for non-VSAM files.

VSAM has its own way of maintaining centralized control over the creation, access and deletion of files. It also manages the DASD space allocated to those files. VSAM accomplishes these tasks by keeping information on file and space characteristics in one place—the VSAM catalog. This catalog facilitates:

1) Keeping track of both files and available DASD space.

2) Writing JCL to create and process VSAM files.

3) Moving VSAM files to other operating systems (for example, DOS to MVS). Another name for this is *system portability*.

Catalogs will be discussed in Chapter 5.

Most readers are familiar with the idea of blocking. Records that make up a file are grouped into physical records or blocks of data. For example, 10 logical records might only result in one physical record or block.

```
FD   MASTER-FILE
     RECORDING MODE IS F
     LABEL RECORDS ARE STANDARD
     RECORD CONTAINS 56 CHARACTERS
     BLOCK CONTAINS 20 RECORDS
```

In this example of a COBOL FD, a fixed-length sequential file is being defined. Each logical record housed on the file contains 56 characters. However, it takes 20 of these records to make up a physical block of data. The latter actually consists of 1,120 characters (multiply record size by blocking factor).

How well you block a file influences performance. Why? A block of data represents the unit of information transmitted across the I/O channel (from the peripheral storage device to the CPU). The poorer a file is blocked, the more times information is passed across the channel. The better it's blocked, the fewer times this time-consuming process occurs. Also, remember that DASD models affect block size. Ask your IBM representative for blocking charts pertaining to the DASD models used by your data center. For example, what's good for a 3340 isn't necessarily good for a 3350.

VSAM files are not blocked. However, they do have an equivalent feature to blocking. Like SAM files, VSAM records must also be transmitted across the I/O channel. The records are stored on DASD but must be available to the CPU when the file is processed.

In VSAM, the records of a data set are grouped into fixed-size units called *control intervals*. The latter are commonly referred to as CIs (see Fig. 1-1).

The CI is the unit of data that VSAM transfers between virtual and peripheral storage. Like blocking factors, CI size has a direct impact on performance. (More about CI size and machine resources in Chapter 9.)

The size of a CI can vary depending on the data set. Sizes range from 512 bytes (.5K) to 32,768 bytes (32K) and must occur in multiples of 512 or 2,048 bytes. Up to 8,192 bytes, CI size must be a multiple of 512; beyond 8K, it must be a multiple of 2,048 (2K). Although CI size can vary by data set, the size within a data set must be consistent (see Fig. 1-2).

Do you have to choose the CI size?

No. VSAM will select a default CI size. Record size and DASD model influence the way VSAM picks the default values of a CI.

On the other hand, you can request a particular CI size. The only requirement is that the size be within the acceptable range of .5K to 32K.

Let's take a quick look at how the CI works in relation to READ statements.

When your program encounters a READ statement, we say that a logical record is being accessed. Since files are stored on such peripheral devices as DASD and magnetic tape, what the READ statement really does is fetch logical records from peripheral storage into virtual storage (in the case of VSAM). However, the computer doesn't keep going back and forth between peripheral and virtual storage for each logical record. When the first record is read on a VSAM file, the entire CI containing that record is read into a VSAM I/O storage buffer in virtual storage. Subsequent READ statements will then retrieve records from the I/O buffer until no more are left in that particular CI. The process is then repeated for the next CI. In other words, an entire CI is read into a VSAM I/O storage buffer, and logical records are then individually retrieved for processing by your program.

CONTROL INTERVALS

The following summarizes the purpose and structure of VSAM control intervals (CIs):

1) Represents units of information that VSAM transfers between peripheral and virtual storage.
2) Contains the records comprising a VSAM data set.
3) CIs are fixed in size within a VSAM data set.
4) Must be stored on contiguous DASD tracks.
5) Varies in size from .5K to 32K.
6) If the size option is not specified, default values will be assumed for the selected DASD model.
7) A CI may span multiple tracks, depending on its size and the track capacity of the DASD model.
8) May contain one or more blocks of data. VSAM will select the best block size in order to make optimum use of the selected DASD model.

FIG. 1-1. Control Intervals

VALID SIZES FOR CIs

Increments of 512 (Up To 8,192 Bytes)		Increments of 2,048 (Over 8,192 Bytes)	
512	4,608	10,240	26,624
1,024	5,120	12,288	28,672
1,536	5,632	14,336	30,720
2,048	6,144	16,384	16,384
2,560	6,656	18,432	32,768
3,072	7,168	20,480	
3,584	7,680	22,528	
4,096	8,192	24,576	

FIG. 1-2. Valid Sizes for CIs

READ statements automatically move individual logical records out of this VSAM I/O buffer. Each record is transferred to a user-defined buffer or work area. By the way, how well you define CI sizes and buffers helps determine how efficiently this process occurs. Space allocated to the VSAM I/O buffer should be large enough to accommodate two or more CIs. The buffer space must be a multiple of the CI size; do not allocate according to the physical record size.

Do you have to calculate buffer size?

No. VSAM can calculate default values for I/O buffer sizes. (More about this later when we discuss AMS).

As programmers, we're primarily concerned with logical records. With code, we define and reference the fields that comprise logical records. In the case of an inventory system, for example, each item in stock typically requires a logical record:

RECORDING MODE IS F

or

RECORDING MODE IS V

These COBOL statements refer respectively to fixed- and variable-length files. IBM supports both formats.

Do you know how the computer distinguishes where variable-length SAM records begin and end?

Each physical block of data is prefixed with a four-byte binary field indicating the size of that particular block. Each logical record in the block is also prefixed with a four-byte binary field. The latter indicates the physical size of the record it is prefixing.

In VSAM, all logical records are treated as though they are variable in length. Like the counterpart of the binary prefix used for variable-length SAM files, VSAM places control fields in each CI to describe the logical records stored in the CI. These control fields are called *record definition fields*, or RDFs. Along with specifying record sizes, an RDF also contains data necessary to locate records stored in the CI.

A logical record in a KSDS or ESDS can span one or more CIs. When a record is stored in this manner, it is called a *spanned record*. (An RRDS cannot contain spanned records.) Spanned records can have a positive impact on DASD usage. They may help reduce DASD requirements for a particular data set, especially when the records comprising it vary significantly in length.

Earlier in this chapter, we introduced the idea of distributed free space. Since a KSDS can have logical records inserted, deleted, lengthened or shortened, DASD space must be allocated for such activities. To be specific, space should be available within the CI to provide for physical size changes experienced by a KSDS.

Free space can be reserved and distributed within CIs. This reservation of free space is under user control (again, more about how to make such allocations when we explore AMS). Free space allocation is specified as a percentage of the CI; for example, 20 percent of a CI may be set aside for free space (Figs. 1-3 and 1-4).

DISTRIBUTED FREE SPACE

The following summarizes the purpose and structure of distributed free space in a VSAM data set:

1) Available only with a KSDS.
2) Represents unused space that appears between the logical records and the RDFs in a CI.
3) Free space size may be reserved in the CI when the data set is loaded to DASD.
4) Used to insert new records or extend records already stored in the CI.
5) Deleted records are automatically reclaimed by VSAM as free space.

FIG. 1-3. Distributed Free Space.

CI STRUCTURE

RECORD 1	RECORD 2	RECORD 3	Free space	CONTROL INTERVAL INFORMATION

FIG. 1-4. Our illustration contains three logical records as well as free space for the storage of additional records. Note that space is also allocated for information related to the CI. An example of such information is the amount of free space available in the CI.

A control field called the *control interval definition* (CIDF) specifies the amount and location of free space available for use within a CI. The CIDF is stored at the very end of a CI. For example, here is a KSDS CI containing two records and distributed free space:

RECORD 1	RECORD 2	Free space	RDF 1	RDF 2	CIDF

CIs don't exist independently of one another. VSAM groups CIs into what are called *control areas*, or CAs. Thus, a VSAM data set consists of one or more CAs (Figs. 1-5 and 1-6).

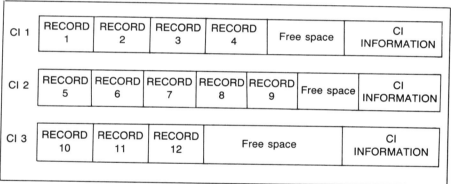

CONTROL AREA   CA STRUCTURE

FIG. 1-5. Our CA contains three control intervals. Note that each CI consists of logical records, free space, and CI information. The entire CA contains 12 logical records.

CONTROL AREAS

The following summarizes the purpose and structure of control areas:

1) Contains multiple CIs.
2) VSAM automatically determines number of CIs stored in a CA.
3) Maximum size allowed for a CA is one DASD cylinder.
4) User defines CA size when specifying the amount of space to be allocated to a data set.
5) May contain free space which user must specify as a percentage of the CA size.

FIG. 1-6. Control Areas

The number of CIs in a CA equals the number of index entries in each index record. Who or what determines this number? VSAM calculates the CA size for you. Both logical record size and DASD model influence the calculation.

FLEXIBILITY

VSAM is a flexible and powerful access method. Some of the advantages afforded by VSAM are:

1) Portability of data sets between operating systems (for example, DOS to MVS).
2) Device independence in regard to DASD models.
3) Centralized control over DASD space management via catalogs.
4) Support of batch and on-line processing.
5) Password capability to protect files from unauthorized access.
6) Provides organizational structures for access to logical records by key, relative address, or relative record number.
7) Reduced need to reorganize files when records are inserted (applicable only to a KSDS).
8) Comprehensive set of AMS utility programs to control, manipulate and monitor data sets.
9) Optimization features for better machine performance.
10) Elimination of programmer concern about physical record size and blocking factors when developing programs.
11) Easy conversion of ISAM files; support for related programs via the IIP.

2
CHAPTER

Key-Sequenced Files

The Key-Sequenced Files (KSDS) Structure is the most widely used VSAM structure. It is also the organizational structure that most closely resembles ISAM.

A KSDS is organized in logical sequence by a key field. Each record contained in the data set has a unique value in the key field. For example, in an inventory system, the key might be the item number.

Keys are not the only way you can reference a KSDS. Records may also be located by address. The latter refers to the byte address of the record relative to the beginning of the data set. The technical term for this is *relative byte address*, or RBA. When this method is used, the index plays no role in the accessing process. Since the RBA method is rarely used nor is it as easy to use, we're going to concentrate our discussion on the indexing feature of a KSDS.

A KSDS can be processed in sequential or direct mode. In either mode, you can add, retrieve, update and delete records. When a KSDS is sequentially accessed, the records are processed one at a time in the order of key values, starting with the record having the lowest value. When random processing is used, your program must supply the value of the key. For example, let's say you wanted to change the reorder date on an item in our Inventory System. Your program would use the item number on the maintenance transaction to access and modify the corresponding master record.

Records contained in a KSDS can also be accessed dynamically. The term *dynamically* means that sequential and/or random access may be mixed for the same file in a given program without having to close and open the file again.

KSDS CLUSTER COMPONENTS

A KSDS cluster consists of two parts:

1) Data component—contains records comprising the file.
2) Index component—contains indexes related to the records in the data component.

The index component of a KSDS consists of one or more levels. Each of these levels is a set of records that contains entries giving the physical location of the records in the next lower level. The lowest level of index records is called a *sequence set*. The latter gives the location of CIs containing the data records. The *index set* refers to the higher level of index records. This set gives the physical location of index records (see Fig. 2-1).

Now, refer to Figs. 2-2 and 2-3 as I explain how VSAM accesses logical records in a KSDS.

In Fig. 2-2, the key is a three-digit item number in an Inventory File. The latter consists of eight CIs; each CI contains

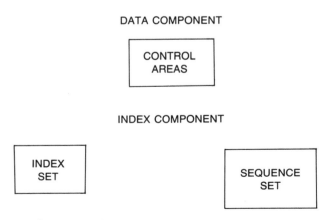

FIG. 2-1. Data Component

four logical records. These records are stored in sequentially ascending order by key value.

The index set contains two entries. Each of these entries contains a pointer to a record in the sequence set along with the value of the highest key indexed by that record.

Each record in the sequence set contains entries for a key and a corresponding CI pointer. These entries represent the value of the highest key contained in that CI.

Using Fig. 2-3, let's see how VSAM goes about locating a specific logical record.

INDEX COMPONENT				
Index Set		Sequence Set		
Key	Sequence Set Pointer	Record	Key	CI Pointer
610	1	1	210	C1
976	2		390	C2
			456	C3
			610	C4
		2	702	C5
			852	C6
			901	C7
			976	C8

FIG. 2-2. The above illustrates the index set and sequence set of an index component.

DATA COMPONENT				
CI	Keys of Records in the CI			
1	120	125	140	210
2	212	265	303	390
3	391	400	401	456
4	520	525	589	610
5	670	696	701	702
6	743	781	830	852
7	871	876	900	901
8	943	960	975	976

FIG. 2-3. The above illustrates the relationship of a CI and logical VSAM records.

The item number is 830. First, the index set is searched for a key greater than or equal to 830. According to our example, this particular key would be indexed in record 2 of the sequence set since 830 is greater than 610 but less than 976.

Next, record 2 of the sequence set is searched for a higher or equal key. A record with a key of 830 would be in CI 6 since the latter contains all records with keys ranging from 743 through 852.

Finally, CI 6 is read and searched sequentially until the desired record is found. As you can see from our sample data component, item number 830 is the third record in CI 6.

ALTERNATE INDEXES

A KSDS provides a special indexing option unique to VSAM. An alternate index (AI) may be defined along with the primary key field(s). For example, an Inventory System may be indexed by item number, but may also have the same vendor name as the AI. Items then could be referenced by either item number or vendor name.

AMS utility programs provide us with the means to define and build alternate indexes. More about this in Chapter 7.

FREE SPACE

The concept of distributed free space was first introduced in Chapter 1. Free space is distributed throughout the KSDS to provide an efficient means of adding and expanding logical records.

When you define a KSDS via AMS commands, you can distribute free space throughout it two ways:

1) Space may be left at the end of all used CIs.
2) Some CIs may be left completely unused.

The amount of free space allocated in a used CI and the number of free CIs in a CA are independent of one another. In other words, both types of free space may be defined. For example, you may specify that 20 percent of the space in each CI and 10

KSDS CA

CONTROL AREA

CI 1	RECORD 1	RECORD 2	RECORD 3	RECORD 4	RECORD 5	CI INFORMATION
CI 2	RECORD 6	RECORD 7	RECORD 8	RECORD 9	RECORD 10	CI INFORMATION
CI 3	Free space					

FIG. 2-4. Example of free space distribution in the data component of a KSDS. Free space can be reserved within each CI, or entire CIs can be left empty. In this illustration, CI 3 has been reserved for free space.

percent of the CIs in each CA be reserved for free space (see Fig. 2-4).

What happens when there is no more free space left in a CI?

Remember how we said that entire CIs can be allocated for free space? To better understand how this works, review the following:

CIs Before Insertion

Item Nbr 520	Item Nbr 525	Item Nbr 570	Item Nbr 587	Item Nbr 588	Item Nbr 610

F R E E S P A C E

CIs After Insertion of Item Nbr 571

Item Nbr 520	Item Nbr 525	Item Nbr 570	Item Nbr 571	FREE SPACE

Item Nbr 587	Item Nbr 588	Item Nbr 610	FREE SPACE

23

In our example, we want to insert a record with a key value of 571 in a CI that has no available free space. Therefore, a *control-interval split* occurs. The record is placed after item number 570, and records 587, 588 and 610 are placed in the free CI, and we thus return to the specified percentage of free space in the original CI. Record insertions and expansions may then use the free space following record 571.

COBOL CONSIDERATIONS

Enough of the physical mechanics of a KSDS! As programmers, we want to know how these data sets can be logically manipulated. To help illustrate our discussion, I've included several examples of COBOL coding.

Environment Division

The following illustrates both requirements and options for the Environment Division when a KSDS is referenced.

```
FILE-CONTROL
    SELECT file-name
    ASSIGN TO system-name
    [ RESERVE integer [AREA / AREAS] ]
    ORGANIZATION IS INDEXED
    [ACCESS MODE IS {SEQUENTIAL / RANDOM / DYNAMIC} ]
    RECORD KEY IS data-name
    [PASSWORD IS data-name]
    [ALTERNATE RECORD KEY IS data-name]
    [PASSWORD IS data-name]
    [WITH DUPLICATES]
    [FILE STATUS IS data-name].
```

In the ASSIGN clause, *system-name* refers to a system logical unit and, optionally, a device class, a device number, and the external name.

SYSnnn[-class][-device][-name]

SYSnnn	Required. Represents the symbolic unit to which the file is assigned. "nnn" must be a three-digit number. Check with your systems programming staff to determine the valid SYS number range for your data center.
class	Optional. "DA" is used to specify DASD files. Treated as documentation.
device	Optional. Treated as documentation.
name	Optional. Specifies the external name by which the file is known to the system. It may be from three to seven characters in length; these may consist of A through Z and 0 through 9. The first character must be alphabetic. If this operand is omitted, the SYS number (SYSnnn) becomes the file's external name.

The RESERVE clause is treated as documentation.

The ORGANIZATION clause specifies the logical structure of the file. When a KSDS is being referenced, a value of INDEXED must be coded.

Records contained in a KSDS can be accessed three ways. The ACCESS MODE clause indicates which option is selected. Valid values are:

1) *Sequential*—Records are accessed in the sequence of ascending record key values.

2) *Random*—Records are accessed according to the key values specified during input/output statements.

3) *Dynamic*—Records are accessed sequentially or randomly, depending on how the input/output requests are coded.

The RECORD KEY clause contains the field name within the KSDS, which contains the key. This clause must be specified for a KSDS, which contains the key. The data name specified in this clause must be defined in the File Section, rather than the Working-Storage Section of the program. The key field's physical location in the program's file description must be the same as that specified when the file was defined via the appropriate AMS utility.

PASSWORD clauses are optional for a KSDS. A PASSWORD clause may follow either the RECORD or ALTERNATE RECORD key clauses, depending on whether it is applicable to the base cluster or the AI. The *data-name* specified in a PASSWORD clause must be defined in the Working-Storage Section as an alphanumeric item. The first eight characters of this field are used as the password; a shorter field is padded with blanks to eight characters. Each password must be equivalent to one that is defined through the appropriate AMS utility when a KSDS is established.

What purpose does a PASSWORD clause serve?

It establishes some security for a KSDS. Access to the file will not be allowed unless a valid password is supplied. (More about passwords in Chapter 10).

An alternative path to the data in a KSDS is specified through the ALTERNATE RECORD KEY clause. Remember our discussion on AIs? For example, it may be desirable to access an Inventory Master via item number or vendor name. The AI provides such flexibility. Records may be randomly accessed by referencing either the RECORD KEY or the ALTERNATE RECORD KEY.

The data name specified in the ALTERNATE RECORD KEY is the field in the file which is used as the KSDS's alternate index. It must be defined as a fixed-length alphanumeric item in the File Section rather than the Working-Storage Section. The physical location of the alternate key's field in the program's file description must be the same as that specified when the file was defined via the appropriate AMS utility. However, the leftmost character position of this field must not be the same as the leftmost character position of the RECORD KEY or of any other ALTERNATE RECORD KEY.

If the DUPLICATES option is specified, the values contained in the ALTERNATE RECORD KEY may be duplicated within any records in the file. When the DUPLICATES option is not specified, the values contained in the ALTERNATE RECORD KEY must be unique among records in the KSDS.

The FILE STATUS clause allows programmers to monitor the execution of each input/output request for the KSDS. Through logic statements referencing the data name specified in the FILE STATUS clause, your program can check to see whether files are opened and closed successfully, whether records are found, when an end-of-file is reached during a sequential read, etc.

The data-name specified in this clause must be defined in the Working-Storage Section of the Data Division as a two-character alphanumeric item. This field must not be defined in the File Section. The field specified in the FILE STATUS clause is automatically updated after execution of each I/O statement for the file.

```
FILE-CONTROL.
    SELECT INV-MASTER
        ASSIGN TO SYS010-DA-3340-INVMST
        ORGANIZATION IS INDEXED
        ACCESS IS SEQUENTIAL
        RECORD KEY IS INV-ITEM-NUMBER
        FILE STATUS IS INV-STATUS-CODE.
DATA DIVISION.
FILE SECTION.
.
.
.

WORKING-STORAGE SECTION.
01  INV-STATUS-CODE          PIC XX.
.
.
.

PROCEDURE DIVISION.
```

010-OPEN-FILES.
>	OPEN INPUT INV-MASTER.
>	IF INV-STATUS-CODE NOT EQUAL 00
>		GO TO 999-ABEND.

Note in our coding example that the status code for the INV-MASTER file is housed in a field called INV-STATUS-CODE. The FILE STATUS clause refers to this field. Every time an I/O action occurs for the INV-MASTER file, the programmer may check to see if the action was successful.

Look at the statement following the OPEN for INV-MASTER:

IF INV-STATUS-CODE NOT EQUAL 00
>	GO TO 999-ABEND.

File status fields contain values indicative of specific file-related conditions. Refer to Appendix A for a detailed explanation of the different values and their associated meanings. If you are going to read, write and/or debug programs referencing VSAM files, it's important that you become familiar with these codes. Although the FILE STATUS clause is optional, we strongly recommend that you use it.

Data Division

The following illustrates both requirements and options for the Data Division when a KSDS is referenced.

FILE SECTION.
FD file-name

$$\left[\text{BLOCK CONTAINS [integer TO] integer} \left\{ \begin{array}{l} \text{CHARACTERS} \\ \text{RECORDS} \end{array} \right\} \right]$$

$$\left[\text{RECORD CONTAINS [integer TO] integer CHARACTERS} \right]$$

$$\text{LABEL} \left\{ \begin{array}{l} \text{RECORD is} \\ \text{RECORDS are} \end{array} \right\} \left\{ \begin{array}{l} \text{STANDARD} \\ \text{OMITTED} \end{array} \right\}$$

$$\left[\text{VALUE OF system-name is} \left\{ \begin{array}{l} \text{Data-name} \\ \text{literal} \end{array} \right\} \right]$$

$$\left[\text{DATA} \left\{ \begin{array}{l} \text{RECORD is} \\ \text{RECORDS are} \end{array} \right\} \text{data-name [data-name]} \ldots \right].$$

Since my purpose is not to teach COBOL but rather to show how VSAM influences the language, I'm not going to explain the nitty-gritty details of each statement above. What I will do is emphasize the VSAM connection.

1) The LABEL RECORD clause is treated solely as documentation. The COBOL compiler, however, requires its presence but does not care whether the STANDARD or OMITTED option is coded.
2) The RECORDING MODE clause is not allowed. (That's why I omitted it from our example!)
3) The BLOCK CONTAINS, DATA RECORDS and VALUE OF clauses are treated solely as documentation.

If you've been used to working with other access methods such as SAM or ISAM, it probably seems strange to suddenly ignore those clauses which have to do with file size. Specifying record size and block size is a way of life for programmers! However, blocking has no meaning for VSAM files; therefore, we don't need the related clauses included in the FD. The CI concept references block size and is controlled through AMS utilities which are external to programs.

Procedure Division

Most of the programming work related to VSAM files is located in this division. In particular, the VSAM influence is present when I/O statements are coded.

First, let's recap what type of operates I/O statements control in relation to files:

1) OPEN
2) CLOSE
3) READ
4) WRITE
5) REWRITE
6) DELETE

Now, we're going to relate each of these I/O statements to VSAM. Also, keep in mind throughout this discussion that each

29

of these I/O statements will automatically update the STATUS KEY if it is defined for the VSAM file. To be on the safe side, you should always check the value of this key after an I/O statement occurs.

$$\text{OPEN} \begin{cases} \text{INPUT file-name [file-name] . . .} \\ \text{OUTPUT file-name [file-name] . . .} \\ \text{I-O file-name [file-name] . . .} \\ \text{EXTEND file-name [file-name] . . .} \end{cases}$$

Multiple files may be referenced in one OPEN statement. In other words, you can open both a SAM and a VSAM file at the same time:

OPEN INV-MASTER CARD-FILE

If a PASSWORD clause is specified in the SELECT statement, the field so noted in the clause must contain the valid password for the cluster being referenced before an OPEN statement can be successfully executed.

When an OPEN INPUT or OPEN I-O statement is encountered for a KSDS, the *current record pointer* is set to the first record physically contained in the file. It starts the program at the physical beginning of a KSDS, and that means the record with the lowest key value.

What if the file is empty? The OPEN statement sets the pointer so that the first READ statement will result in an AT END (end-of-file) condition.

A few words about the EXTEND option. It permits opening the KSDS for output operations only, and ACCESS MODE SEQUENTIAL must be specified in the SELECT statement. When EXTEND is coded, the OPEN statement prepares the file for the addition of new records immediately following the last record in the KSDS. By the way, the last record on file is the one with the highest key value when a KSDS is involved.

IDENTIFICATION DIVISION.

.

.

.

```
ENVIRONMENT DIVISION.
    .
    .
    .
FILE-CONTROL.

    SELECT INV-MASTER
        ASSIGN TO SYS010-DA-3340-INVMST
        ORGANIZATION IS INDEXED
        ACCESS IS SEQUENTIAL
        RECORD KEY IS INV-ITEM-NUMBER
        FILE STATUS IS INV-STATUS-CODE.
    .
    .
    .
DATA DIVISION.
FILE SECTION.
FD   INV-MASTER
        LABEL RECORDS ARE STANDARD.
01   INV-REC.
     05   INV-ITEM-NUMBER            PIC S9(6).
     05   INV-VENDOR                 PIC X (30).
     05  INV-ITEM-DESC               PIC X(25).
     05   INV-LAST-ORDER-DATE        PIC S9(6).
WORKING-STORAGE SECTION.
01   INV-STATUS-CODE                 PIC XX.
    .
    .
    .
PROCEDURE DIVISION.
010-OPEN-FILES.
    OPEN EXTEND INV-MASTER.
    IF INV-STATUS-CODE NOT EQUAL 00
        GO TO 999-ABEND.
```

In this example, we opened the KSDS in the EXTEND mode. Note that in our SELECT statement, we coded ACCESS IS SEQUENTIAL; the latter is necessary to use the EXTEND option.

Also, notice that a partial file layout is given for INV-MASTER. The key field is INV-ITEM-NUMBER and is so specified in the RECORD KEY clause. Although we defined INV-ITEM-NUMBER at the physical beginning of the file, such placement is not necessary. In other words, INV-ITEM-NUMBER could start at byte 50 and still serve as the key field.

CLOSE file-name   [WITH LOCK]
     [file-name   [WITH LOCK]] . . .

One CLOSE statement may be used to reference multiple files. Furthermore, there are no restrictions as to mixing access modes. For example, two SAM files and one VSAM file may be referenced in the same statement:

CLOSE CARD-FILE
     PRINT-FILE
     INV-MASTER.

LOCK is the only option available for VSAM files. If it is present, the file cannot be opened again during the current execution of the program.

Before moving on to discuss the READ verb, let's look at START and INVALID KEY statements. Both can play important roles when you're trying to access records contained in a KSDS.

START file-name   [KEY is $\begin{Bmatrix} \text{EQUAL TO} \\ \text{GREATER THAN} \\ \text{NOT LESS THAN} \end{Bmatrix}$ data-name]

[INVALID KEY imperative-statement]

With the START statement, you can achieve a logical positioning within a KSDS. So, let's say you want to read the file sequentially starting at key 2500. Rather than wasting resources sequentially reading the records on file up to the one with a key value of 2500, use the START statement. By referencing the KSDS index, the START statement can position the current record pointer at a specific record or a specific area. (When we use the term "area," we're thinking in terms of the GREATER THAN or NOT LESS THAN options.) Starting at this location, records may then be sequentially retrieved with subsequent READ statements.

When the START statement is used, the associated KSDS must be opened in the INPUT or I-O mode. The ACCESS MODE clause in the SELECT statement must be defined with SEQUENTIAL or DYNAMIC access.

What if the KEY option is omitted?

The EQUAL TO relational operator is implied if the KEY option is not specified:

```
FILE-CONTROL.
    SELECT INV-MASTER
        ASSIGN TO SYS010-DA-3340-INVMST
        ORGANIZATION IS INDEXED
        ACCESS IS SEQUENTIAL
        RECORD KEY IS INV-ITEM-NUMBER
        FILE STATUS IS INV-STATUS-CODE.
    .
    .
    .

PROCEDURE DIVISION.
010-OPEN-FILES.
    .
    .
    .

020-START-RTN.
MOVE 2500 TO INV-ITEM-NUMBER.
START INV-MASTER
        KEY IS GREATER INV-ITEM-NUMBER
        INVALID KEY GO TO 999-ABEND.
```

Using this COBOL example for reference, note that the data-name used in the START statement's relational operator is the same as that specified in the RECORD KEY clause. When the START statement is executed, a comparison is made between the current value in the key field's data-name and the corresponding key field in the KSDS. In this case, the current record pointer would be positioned at the record with a key greater than 2500.

What if the comparison test can't be satisfied? Let's say that the highest item number on file is 2350. We now have an INVALID KEY condition; the current record pointer doesn't know where to go. Now you know why COBOL provides an INVALID KEY clause. Although optional, I strongly recommend that you take advantage of it.

In other words, if the comparison test fails, an error condition exists. Learn to recognize such errors and hopefully avoid unnecessary program abends. Furthermore, since an error condition occurs if the test isn't met, it is wise to avoid EQUAL TO comparisons; consider using the GREATER THAN test instead.

The INVALID KEY clause isn't limited to the START verb. It's also available with the WRITE, REWRITE and DELETE verbs. However, I recommend checking the FILE STATUS field, rather than using the INVALID KEY statement, when dealing with any verb other than START. VSAM'S FILE STATUS testing capability is quite involved and provides you with the opportunity to check for all possible I/O conditions. Besides, anytime sequential access is used, you're not supposed to use the INVALID KEY statement; it was initially designed with direct access in mind. When VSAM came along, the idea further evolved into FILE STATUS checking.

What happens when an INVALID KEY condition occurs?

If an INVALID KEY statement is not included in the program, processing will pass to the first statement following the START and continue from there. However, this action may result in serious problems since the current record pointer is not correctly positioned.

If an INVALID KEY statement is present, processing will pass to the statements following the words "INVALID KEY":

```
INVALID KEY GO TO 999-ABEND
READ . . .
```

In this example, processing would go to the 999-ABEND paragraph if an INVALID KEY condition occurred; otherwise, a READ statement would be invoked. In 999-ABEND, you could then logically handle the erroneous condition by displaying explanatory messages, aborting the program, etc. The START statement can also be followed by a FILE STATUS test rather than an INVALID KEY statement.

SEQUENTIAL RETRIEVAL

    READ file-name [NEXT] RECORD [INTO identifier]

        [AT END imperative-statement]

RANDOM RETRIEVAL

    READ file-name RECORD [INTO identifier]

        [KEY IS data-name]

        INVALID KEY imperative-statement]

There are two different formats available for READ statements referencing a KSDS. For sequential access, the READ statement makes available the next logical record on file. For random access, the READ statement makes available a specific record.

If ACCESS MODE SEQUENTIAL is specified (or assumed as a default), READ statements must subscribe to the sequential format. The random format will be used if ACCESS MODE RANDOM is coded.

When it comes to the DYNAMIC mode, however, the rules are slightly more involved:

    1) Either sequential or random record retrieval may be specified.

    2) If the sequential format is used, the NEXT option must be included.

    3) When records are to be randomly retrieved, the random format must be used.

```
READ INV-MASTER.
IF INV-STATUS-CODE NOT EQUAL 00
    GO TO 999-ABEND.
```

The sequential format is used in this example. Also, note that we checked the FILE STATUS field, rather than coding an INVALID KEY condition.

```
FILE-CONTROL.
    SELECT INV-MASTER
        ASSIGN TO SYS010-DA-3340-INVMST
        ORGANIZATION IS INDEXED
        ACCESS IS RANDOM
        RECORD KEY IS INV-ITEM-NUMBER
        FILE STATUS IS INV-STATUS-CODE.
.
.
.
    MOVE 1023 TO INV-ITEM-NUMBER.
    READ INV-MASTER
        KEY IS INV-ITEM-NUMBER.
    IF INV-STATUS-CODE NOT EQUAL 00
        GO TO 999-ABEND.
```

Here, the record with a key value of 1023 will be directly retrieved. Although we included the KEY clause, it is optional. Random reads can be very handy, especially when writing file maintenance programs. As long as the file's key field is also available on the maintenance transaction level, the maintenance file can be sequentially read while randomly applying the updates to the master. Furthermore, the FILE STATUS field can be checked for such conditions as missing master records:

```
IF INV-STATUS-CODE-EQUAL 23
    PERFORM 700-MISSING-MASTER.
```

This time, we checked for the specific value of 23. When a READ statement is executed, a resulting value of 23 indicates that the desired record cannot be found. (For a more detailed explanation of file status codes, refer to Appendix A.)

```
FILE-CONTROL.
    SELECT INV-MASTER
    ASSIGN TO SYS010-DA-3340-INVMST
    ORGANIZATION IS INDEXED
    ACCESS IS DYNAMIC
    RECORD KEY IS INV-ITEM-NUMBER
```

```
          FILE STATUS IS INV-STATUS-CODE.
  .
  .
  .

      MOVE 1109 TO INV-ITEM-NUMBER.
      READ INV-MASTER.
  .
  .
  .

      MOVE 1954 TO INV-ITEM-NUMBER.
      START INV-MASTER
          KEY = INV-TEM-NUMBER.
      READ INV-MASTER NEXT.
```

When DYNAMIC access is used, records may be retrieved either sequentially or randomly. Note that NEXT was used in the sequential format.

WRITE record-name [FROM identifier]

[INVALID KEY imperative-statement]

The WRITE statement releases a logical record to a file which has been opened as OUTPUT, I-O, or EXTEND. When the record is physically written to the file, its accompanying index entry is also created, the value of which is based on the contents of the key field. In our on-going example, that's INV-ITEM-NBR.

What if a record already exists on file with the key you're trying to add?

VSAM protects you from this potentially disastrous situation. By checking the FILE STATUS code, you can determine if the WRITE statement encountered this particular problem:

```
IF INV-STATUS-CODE EQUAL 22
    PERFORM 800-DUPLICATE-REC.
```

A WRITE statement resulting in a FILE STATUS value of 22 is indicative of a duplicate key condition.

```
WRITE INV-MASTER-REC.
IF INV-STATUS-CODE NOT EQUAL 00
    PERFORM 500-DISPLAY-ERRORS.
```

Note that the INVALID KEY option is omitted in favor of checking the FILE STATUS. Take my advice and do the same!

REWRITE record-name [FROM identifier]

[INVALID KEY imperative-statement]

The REWRITE statement is used to logically modify an existing record already on file. To use the REWRITE statement, the associated file must be opened as I-O.

When ACCESS MODE SEQUENTIAL is specified, the record to be modified (or, rather, physically replaced) is the one retrieved by the last sequential READ. The value of the field specified as the RECORD KEY must remain unchanged. In other words, you can't modify key fields and then attempt to REWRITE records. Also, remember that the length of the record can't be changed through a REWRITE statement.

When random or dynamic access is specified, the data item defined as the key field must contain the key for the record you wish to REWRITE. Under these access modes, however, the record does not have to be processed by a READ statement first. Depending on what you are trying to accomplish, though, it might be advisable to READ the record first. For example, in a file maintenance program, you might wish to print a report showing the values of fields before and after changes occur.

```
MOVE 1921 TO INV-ITEM-NBR.
REWRITE INV-MASTER-REC.
IF INV-STATUS-CODE NOT EQUAL 00
    PERFORM . . .
```

In this example of the REWRITE statement, an access mode of RANDOM or DYNAMIC has been specified. How do we know this? A value of 1921 is being moved to the record key, and thus a READ statement is unnecessary. The appropriate record is accessed through the RECORD KEY field.

DELETE file-name RECORD

[INVALID KEY imperative-statement]

The DELETE statement is used to logically remove specific records from a KSDS. Before this can occur, however, the file must have been opened as I-O.

If ACCESS MODE SEQUENTIAL has been specified in the SELECT statement, the last prior I/O statement for the associated file must be a successfully executed READ. Then, when the DELETE statement is executed, the system logically removes the record retrieved by that READ statement.

By the way, one important rule to remember—the INVALID KEY option cannot follow a DELETE verb when sequential access is used. When the DELETE statement is used on a file in the random or dynamic mode, the system logically removes the record identified by the contents of the associated RECORD KEY.

```
MOVE 3612 TO INV-ITEM-NBR.
DELETE INV-MASTER
```

Under random or dynamic access mode, a specific record can be deleted without ever being read. In our example, the record with a key value of 3612 will be physically removed from the KSDS.

Once a DELETE statement is successfully executed, the record is logically gone. It can no longer be accessed by a program.

ALTERNATE INDEX AND COBOL

Before leaving our discussion on the KSDS, I want to include a few key points about AIs and the COBOL language. This is not an in-depth presentation on this particular topic; for that, I refer you to your IBM library manuals, some of which are listed in the Bibliography.

A KSDS is not required to have an alternate index. Perhaps there is only one way you wish to access a file. In such instances, do not specify an ALTERNATE RECORD KEY in the SELECT statement. Like the primary index, AIs are also established via

AMS utilities and are then utilized through program logic statements.

Along with establishing the alternate record key, accessing a file in an alternate sequence requires specification of the alternate key with which processing is to begin. You can accomplish this by moving a value to the field specified as the alternate record key and then using the START verb:

```
FILE-CONTROL.
    SELECT INV-MASTER
        ASSIGN TO SYS010-DA-3340-INVMST
        ORGANIZATION IS INDEXED
        ACCESS IS DYNAMIC
        RECORD KEY IS INV-ITEM-NUMBER
        ALTERNATE RECORD KEY IS INV-VENDOR
        FILE STATUS IS INV-STATUS-CODE.
    .
    .
    .
PROCEDURE DIVISION.
    .
    .
    .
    MOVE TRANS-VENDOR TO INV-VENDOR.
    START INV-MASTER KEY = INV-VENDOR
        INVALID KEY MOVE 1 TO WS-KEY ERROR.
```

The ALTERNATE RECORD KEY is a field named INV-VENDOR. Here, we moved the value housed in another field (TRANS-VENDOR) to the data-name for the alternate key field. We could have just as easily written this statement:

```
MOVE 'WAVA & COMPANY' TO INV-VENDOR.
```

In either case, the next READ statement will retrieve the record with an alternate record key value equal to the value housed in the data-name INV-VENDOR.

Regardless of whether you're dealing with primary or alternate keys, the same rules and options apply to the START verb.

Random processing with alternate indexes provides you with the capability to retrieve a record by either a primary key or an alternate key. Don't forget that multiple alternate keys may be defined for a KSDS. The value of whichever key you use must be placed in the appropriate key field prior to the READ statement. The WRITE, REWRITE and DELETE verbs are associated with only the prime RECORD KEY. Only the READ statement may be used in connection with an alternate index.

Unlike primary keys, alternate keys may be changed on existing records. A new value is simply moved into the alternate record key field; VSAM then automatically updates the alternate index so that the record can be accessed by its new AI.

```
MOVE TRANS-VENDOR TO INV-VENDOR.
READ INV-MASTER-FILE
    KEY IS INV-VENDOR.
```

This READ statement will allow us to randomly access INV-MASTER-FILE. The value housed in the data-name TRANS-VENDOR has been moved to INV-VENDOR (which is an alternate index for this particular file). When you use random retrieval and an AI, you must use the KEY option to specify that the alternate index key is being used as the key of reference. If you do not specify a KEY option, the primary record key is assumed. That could get you in a great deal of trouble, especially if a value hasn't even been moved to the key field!

3
CHAPTER

Entry-Sequenced Files

The Entry-Sequenced Files (ESDS) structure is often referred to as a VSAM Sequential File. Records cannot be directly accessed via a primary key since there is no indexing available under ESDS.

An ESDS is organized in logical and physical sequence by the way records are read in when the file is initially created. The following Inventory Log File illustrates this concept.

Item Nbr	Tran Code	Order Date
1319	20	110186
1430	20	110186
2375	30	110286
1215	20	110186
3344	30	110486
2218	30	110286
1001	20	110186

There is no ascending or descending sequencing scheme to these records. If in fact they are read into the program in such a sequence, this is exactly the way they will be written to the ESDS. Thus, the fourth record in this ESDS will be item number 1215.

How useful can an organizational structure be which maintains records in the physical sequence in which they are written into the file?

Actually, that's a pretty fair description of SAM files. Why then do so many in the DP profession regard the ESDS as a limited organizational structure? Probably because when we think of VSAM, we see it as ISAM's high-powered replacement, and therefore as an access method allowing for the easy direct retrieval of records.

There are applications where the ESDS is useful. It's appropriate for applications which require no particular ordering of data according to the contents of records. For example, ESDS is well-suited to store a log file in which the order of records corresponds to a sequence of events. New records will continually be added to the end of the ESDS until it is totally rewritten as a new physical cluster (or data set space is exceeded).

I've repeatedly associated the term *sequential* with the ESDS structure, so is sequentially the only way you can access such a file?

No. (Realize, however, that the easiest way to access an ESDS is sequentially, even though direct capability is available.) An ESDS can be processed in sequential or direct mode. In either mode, you can add, retrieve and update records. Note that neither mode affords a way to delete records. Like SAM files, the ESDS must be physically rewritten as a separate file in order to remove records.

Since there is no prime index (as in the case of a KSDS) associated with an ESDS, the programmer is responsible for developing indexing schemes which allow direct processing. When you place a record in an ESDS, VSAM stores a relative byte address (RBA) with the record. The RBA indicates each record's displacement in bytes from the beginning of the file. For example, if the records are 50 bytes long, the first record's RBA is zero because it starts at the beginning of the file. The RBA of the second record is then 50; the third, 100; the fourth, 150; etc.

To access an ESDS directly, you must know the record's RBA. Tracking can be kept by keeping a cross-reference table or file used solely for indexing purposes. In the case of an Inventory File, such tables or files would associate the item number with the RBA.

Is it easier to use a KSDS? If direct processing is desired, we think the KSDS is much better. Too much of the work falls on the programmer's shoulders when attempts are made to access an ESDS directly. It was designed for sequential processing and is best left to that.

ESDS CLUSTER COMPONENTS

An ESDS cluster consists of only a data component that contains records comprising the file.

ALTERNATE INDEXES

An AI may be associated with an ESDS. AMS utility programs provide a means to define and build alternate indexes.

However, this particular organizational structure does not easily lend itself to any type of indexing, whether primary or alternate. Therefore, I have elected to limit our discussion to the sequential accessing of an ESDS.

FREE SPACE

Free space is not distributed throughout an ESDS because there is no need for it. Free space, if you'll recall, is used by a KSDS to facilitate the insertion and expansion of logical records. Since records can only be added to the end of an ESDS, it's unnecessary to allocate room for them elsewhere in the file. Also, records housed in an ESDS cannot be expanded; they may be variable in length, but once entered cannot be changed (Fig. 3-1).

ESDS CA

CONTROL AREA

CI 1	RECORD 1	RECORD 2	RECORD 3	RECORD 4	RECORD 5	CI INFORMATION
CI 2	RECORD 6	RECORD 7	RECORD 8	RECORD 9	RECORD 10	CI INFORMATION
CI 3	RECORD 11	RECORD 12	Free space			

FIG. 3-1. Example of an ESDS CA. Additional records must be added after the last record already on file. Note that in our illustration, free space for such additions follows logical record 12.

COBOL CONSIDERATIONS

Numerous illustrations of the relationship between COBOL and VSAM were presented in Chapter 2. Although the three VSAM organizational structures share many programming features, there are differences. In the next several pages, I'll discuss how the ESDS structure influences COBOL coding.

Environment Division

The following illustrates both requirements and options for the Environment Division when an ESDS is referenced.

FILE-CONTROL.

SELECT [OPTIONAL] file-name

ASSIGN TO system-name

[RESERVE integer $\begin{bmatrix} AREA \\ AREAS \end{bmatrix}$

[ORGANIZATION IS SEQUENTIAL]

[ACCESS MODE IS SEQUENTIAL]

[PASSWORD IS data-name]

[FILE STATUS IS data-name].

The OPTIONAL clause might be a new feature for you. It must be specified for input files that are not necessarily present each time the program is executed.

In the ASSIGN clause, system-name refers to a system logical unit and, optionally, a device class, a device number, the file organization, and the external name.

SYSnnn–class–device–AS–name

SYSnnn Required. Represents the symbolic unit to which the file is assigned. "nnn" must be a three-digit number. Check with your systems programming staff to determine the valid SYS number range for your data center.

class Optional. Treated as documentation.

device Optional. Treated as documentation.

AS   Refers to the organization type; must be specified when the file is an ESDS.

name   Optional. Specifies the external name by which the file is known to the system. It may be from three to seven characters in length; these may consist of A through Z and 0 through 9. The first character must be alphabetic. If this operand is omitted, the SYS number (SYSnnn) becomes the file's external name.

The RESERVE clause is treated as documentation.

The ORGANIZATION clause specifies the logical structure of the file. When an ESDS is being referenced, a value of SEQUENTIAL must be coded.

An ACCESS MODE of SEQUENTIAL must be coded for an ESDS. Records are accessed sequentially by the way they are physically loaded to the file.

PASSWORD support is an optional feature for an ESDS. The data-name specified in a PASSWORD clause must be defined in the Working-Storage Section as an alphanumeric item. The first eight characters of this field are used as the password; a shorter field is padded with blanks to eight characters. The password must be equivalent to the one that is defined through the appropriate AMS utility when an ESDS is established.

This security feature of VSAM may be used to restrict access to some or all of your files. Password-protected files cannot be opened unless valid passwords are supplied. (More about this optional feature in Chapter 10.)

The FILE STATUS clause provides you with a way to monitor the execution of each I/O statement. By adding code in your program which references the data-name specified in the FILE STATUS clause, it can logically be determined whether files are opened and closed successfully, when an end-of-file is reached during a sequential read, when attempts are made to read files not opened, etc.

The data-name specified in this clause must be defined in the Working-Storage Section of the Data Division as a two-character alphanumeric item. This field must not be defined in the File Section. The field specified in the FILE STATUS clause is automatically updated after execution of each I/O statement for the file.

```
FILE-CONTROL.
    SELECT INV-MASTER
        ASSIGN TO SYS010-DA-3340-AS-INVMST
        ORGANIZATION IS SEQUENTIAL
        ACCESS IS SEQUENTIAL
        FILE STATUS IS INV-STATUS-CODE.

DATA DIVISION.
FILE SECTION.
.
.
.

WORKING-STORAGE SECTION.
01   INV-STATUS-CODE          PIC XX.
.
.
.

PROCEDURE DIVISION.
.
.
.

100-READ-MASTER.
    READ INV-MASTER
        AT END GO TO 900-CLOSE-FILES.
    IF INV-STATUS-CODE NOT EQUAL 00
        GO TO 999-ABEND.
```

As you can see from this example, the status code for the INV-MASTER file is a field called INV-STATUS-CODE. Each I/O action related to the INV-MASTER file updates INV-STATUS-CODE with a numeric value. By checking this field for specific values, you can determine through program logic whether I/O commands are successfully executed.

Here are two general rules regarding FILE STATUS codes:

1) Always include a FILE STATUS code when dealing with a VSAM file.

2) When checking the value of a FILE STATUS code, a value other than zero usually signifies an abnormal condition. Realize, however, that "abnormal condition" includes conditions such as end-of-files and duplicate keys. In other words, a value other than zero doesn't necessarily mean disaster, but does always deserve special attention.

Data Division

The following illustrates both requirements and options for the Data Division when an ESDS is referenced:

FILE SECTION.

FD file-name

$$\left[\text{BLOCK CONTAINS [integer TO] integer} \left\{ \begin{matrix} \text{CHARACTERS} \\ \text{RECORDS} \end{matrix} \right\} \right]$$

[RECORD CONTAINS [integer TO] integer CHARACTERS]

$$\text{LABEL} \left\{ \begin{matrix} \text{RECORD is} \\ \text{RECORDS are} \end{matrix} \right\} \left\{ \begin{matrix} \text{STANDARD} \\ \text{OMITTED} \end{matrix} \right\}$$

$$\left[\text{VALUE OF system-name is} \left\{ \begin{matrix} \text{data-name} \\ \text{literal} \end{matrix} \right\} \right]$$

$$\left[\text{DATA} \left\{ \begin{matrix} \text{RECORD is} \\ \text{RECORDS are} \end{matrix} \right\} \text{data-name [data-name] . . .} \right] .$$

As I explained earlier, my goal isn't to teach you COBOL but simply to relate the language to VSAM. Every access method influences every language capable of supporting it. The two elements of any language where access method influence is most visible are *file descriptions* and *I/O verbs*.

When coding an FD for an ESDS, keep in mind the following rules:

1) The COBOL compiler treats the LABEL RECORD clause as documentation only. Although its presence is required, it does not make any difference whether the LABEL RECORD clause is coded with the STANDARD or OMITTED option.

2) It's invalid to include the RECORDING MODE clause. Note that we did not include one in our example.

3) The BLOCK CONTAINS, DATA RECORDS and VALUE OF clauses may be included, but the COBOL compiler treats them as documentation only.

Why don't we need record and block size specifications?

Record and block sizes are dealt with through AMS utilities when VSAM files are involved. We'll talk more about AMS later. Furthermore, VSAM's CI concept replaces blocking.

Procedure Division

Let's take a look at how the following I/O statements are influenced by an ESDS:

1) OPEN
2) CLOSE
3) READ
4) WRITE
5) REWRITE

Did you notice that we omitted one I/O operation which was discussed in relationship to a KSDS?

We didn't include a DELETE statement. Records cannot be deleted from an ESDS unless a new file is written. It's impossible to delete a record from an existing ESDS.

As we discuss each I/O statement and relate it to an ESDS, remember the importance of using FILE STATUS codes. If the latter are included, the I/O statement will automatically update the code. This code can then be checked, using program logic statements, to determine the status of the ESDS following the I/O operation. For example, checking the FILE STATUS code for a value of 10 is how you determine when an end-of-file is reached.

$$\text{OPEN} \begin{cases} \text{INPUT file-name [file-name]} \dots \\ \text{OUTPUT file-name [file-name]} \dots \\ \text{I/O file-name [file-name]} \dots \\ \text{EXTEND file-name [file-name]} \dots \end{cases}$$

More than one file may be referenced in an OPEN statement. For example, two SAM files may be opened or two SAM files and one VSAM file:

```
OPEN   INV-MASTER
       PRINT-FILE
       CARD-FILE.
```

If a PASSWORD clause is specified in the SELECT statement, the field referenced by this clause must contain the valid password for the cluster being referenced; otherwise, the OPEN statement cannot be successfully executed.

By the way, do you realize that a PASSWORD field can be loaded with a valid value several different ways?

1) Code the PASSWORD field using the VALUE clause.

2) Prompt the operator for a value and then move it to the PASSWORD field.

3) Read another file, moving a value from it to the PASSWORD field.

The OPEN INPUT or OPEN I-O statement sets the current record pointer to the first record physically contained in the file. If the file is empty, the first READ statement will result in an AT END (end-of-file) condition.

An ESDS is initially built by using the OPEN OUTPUT statement. The file is then physically written in the same order as its input records are read in.

The EXTEND option allows you to add records to the end of an ESDS once it is created. When the program opens a file using this option, it automatically moves the current record pointer past the records already stored. WRITE is the only I/O statement that can be used when the EXTEND option is selected.

CLOSE file-name [WITH LOCK]

    [file-name [WITH LOCK]] . . .

Multiple files may be referenced with one CLOSE statement. Also, you can mix access methods. For example, in one CLOSE statement you can reference a VSAM file and a SAM file.

CLOSE INV-MASTER CARD-FILE.

LOCK is the only option available when referencing VSAM files. If the LOCK option is present, the file cannot be opened again during the current execution of the program.

In Chapter 2, I preceded the discussion of the READ statement with an introduction to the START and INVALID KEY statements. Although both play major roles during the accessing of records from a KSDS, neither the START nor INVALID KEY statements are supported for ESDS processing.

Think about this for a moment. Why doesn't COBOL recognize either of these statements for an ESDS? Both START and INVALID KEY statements are dependent on record key logic, and an ESDS does not have record keys.

READ file-name RECORD [INTO identifier]

    [AT END imperative-statement]

There is only one format available when coding a READ statement for an ESDS. Why do you need more than one? The only way an ESDS can be read is sequentially, starting with the first physical record on file.

READ INV-MASTER.
IF INV-STATUS-CODE EQUAL 10
    GO TO 900-CLOSE-FILES.

In this example of the READ statement, we checked the FILE STATUS code for a value of 10. If you'll refer to Appendix A, you'll see that a value of 10 indicates that an end-of-file condition has been reached.

WRITE record-name [FROM identifier]

The WRITE statement is used to release a logical record to a physical file. In the case of an ESDS, records must be written in the sequential mode. In other words, a record added to an ESDS must follow the previous record added to the file.

```
WRITE INV-MASTER-REC.
IF INV-STATUS-CODE NOT EQUAL 00
    PERFORM 500-DISPLAY-ERRORS.
```

Here, the WRITE statement added a record to the current end-of-file for INV-MASTER. The INV-STATUS-CODE was then checked to determine whether the I/O operation was successfully executed.

REWRITE record-name [FROM identifier]

The REWRITE statement allows you to logically modify an existing record. In order to use the REWRITE statement, the associated file must be opened as I-O. However, you cannot change the physical size of a record by rewriting it.

```
010-0PEN-FILES.
    OPEN I-O INV-MASTER.
    .
    .
    .

    READ INV-MASTER.
    IF INV-STATUS-CODE NOT EQUAL 00
        GO TO 500-DISPLAY-ERRORS.
    .
    .
    .

    REWRITE INV-MASTER-REC.
    IF INV-STATUS-CODE NOT EQUAL 00
            GO TO 500-DISPLAY-ERRORS.
    .
    .
    .

900-CLOSE-FILES.
    CLOSE INV-MASTER.
```

The REWRITE statement was used to modify the contents of a record(s) housed on INV-MASTER. (Actually, only those records being modified need to be rewritten. The others will continue to remain as they are—unchanged.) Again, *always* check the FILE STATUS code when an I/O operation occurs.

4
CHAPTER

Relative-Record Files

A popular way to describe a Relative-Record File (RRDS) is to say that it is a structure of fixed-length slots that contain records. Each slot is assigned a relative record number; these numbers start at 1, and incrementing by 1 go up to the maximum number of records that can be stored in the file. Thus, a record's physical placement in an RRDS is relative to the slot number it has been assigned.

The slot number concept will recur in this discussion of the RRDS structure.

A record contained in an RRDS is identified (by that, I mean stored and retrieved) in accordance with the relative record number of the slot. As you'll shortly discover, a RELATIVE KEY clause in the COBOL SELECT statement is used to communicate this number.

Like the other VSAM structures, records in an RRDS are grouped together in CIs. Each CI for a specific file contains the same number of fixed-length slots (see Fig. 4-1).

Did you notice that I described these slots as being *fixed-length*?

An RRDS can contain only fixed-length records. In other words, every slot is exactly the same size. When variable-length records are involved, the slots are as long as the longest record in the file. Therefore, you may expand any record on file to the maximum length. Since every slot is the same size, a slot may

VSAM RRDS

CONTROL AREA

CI 1				
RECORD 1	RECORD 2	SLOT 3 (free)	RECORD 4	SLOT 5 (free)
CI 2				
SLOT 6 (free)	SLOT 7 (free)	RECORD 8	RECORD 9	RECORD 10
CI 3				
RECORD 11	RECORD 12	SLOT 13 (free)	RECORD 14	SLOT 15 (free)

FIG. 4-1. VSAM RRDS

contain unused space if variable-length records are involved. Therefore, in the true technical sense, each record is fixed in length.

Does an RRDS have an index?

No. When RRDS records are inserted, modified or deleted, they are referenced by their relative record numbers rather than by an index. The relative record number may be assigned when a record is added to an RRDS, or you can allow VSAM to simply assign it the next available number.

Three access modes are supported:

1) *Sequential*—Records are accessed in sequentially ascending order according to relative record numbers.

2) *Random*—Program logic controls the sequence in which records are accessed. The RELATIVE KEY clause (which I'll shortly elaborate on more) is required. A specific record may be accessed by placing its relative record number in the RELATIVE KEY field.

3) *Dynamic*—By using the appropriate formats for I/O statements, access may be changed from sequential to random within a given program. Any number of sequential and/or random accesses is allowed. In other words, you may have four

sequential READs, then three random READs, and then another sequential READ.

VSAM accesses an RRDS either directly or sequentially. VSAM does not permit you to retrieve a record based on its relative byte address (RBA). An RRDS is physically organized in such a way that VSAM can calculate the address of the CI that contains the requested record. It then calculates the requested record's position within the CI. When an RRDS is processed sequentially, we say that the data records are accessed in sequential order, starting with slot number 1. However, any empty slots are automatically skipped during sequential processing.

The RRDS structure is better for fixed-length records than variable-length records. We say this primarily because the slots must all be the same size, and therefore variable-length records result in unused file space.

Let's relate our ongoing example of an Inventory System to the RRDS.

In the case of our Inventory File, the item number can be used as the relative record number. As long as the latter is unique, it may be used to reference a slot. What we've really done is use the relative record number like a KSDS RECORD KEY clause. Records can be located as through they are in a KSDS but without the time it takes to search the index of a KSDS.

However, don't be fooled into believing that the RRDS structure is always the best answer when direct processing is desired. For example, alternate index keys are not supported. Also, a DELETE does not result in the record's space being physically reclaimed. To be reused, a record must be moved into the deleted space using exactly the same relative record number as the one previously stored there.

When you use an RRDS, you pretty well have to know that you'll be satisfied referencing records either sequentially or by a pre-established range of slot numbers. You can't just change relative record numbers at will!

RRDS CLUSTER COMPONENTS

An RRDS cluster consists of only a data component that contains records comprising the file.

ALTERNATE INDEXES

AIs are not supported for an RRDS.

FREE SPACE

Free space is not distributed throughout an RRDS. CIs are broken down into slots, and each slot is assigned a relative record number. Whether or not slots are used or remain empty depends on program logic and input data.

Records may be added to the end of an RRDS as long as free slots are available. They may also be inserted wherever free slots exist.

COBOL CONSIDERATIONS

In the last two chapters, I've included several illustrations showing you how VSAM structures can affect COBOL coding rules. One obvious point (we hope by now!) is that the three VSAM structures themselves vary in how they influence COBOL. In the next several pages, I'll show you how the RRDS structure impacts COBOL.

Environment Division

The following illustrates both requirements and options for the Environment Division when an RRDS is referenced.

FILE-CONTROL.
    SELECT file-name
    ASSIGN to system-name
    [RESERVE integer $\begin{bmatrix} \text{AREA} \\ \text{AREAS} \end{bmatrix}$]
    ORGANIZATION is RELATIVE

$$\left[\text{ACCESS MODE is}\left\{\begin{array}{l}\text{SEQUENTIAL [RELATIVE KEY}\\ \quad \text{is data-name]}\\ \left\{\begin{array}{l}\text{RANDOM}\\ \text{DYNAMIC} \quad \text{RELATIVE KEY}\\ \quad\quad\quad \text{is data-name}\end{array}\right.\end{array}\right\}\right]$$

[PASSWORD is data-name].
[FILE STATUS is data-name].

In the ASSIGN clause, system-name refers to a system logical unit and, optionally, a device class, a device number, and the external name.

SYSnnn [-class][-device][-name]

SYSnnn   Required. Represents the symbolic unit to which the file is assigned. "nnn" must be a three-digit number. Check with your systems programming staff to determine the valid SYS number range for your data center.

class   Optional. Treated as documentation.
device   Optional. Treated as documentation.
name   Optional. Specifies the external name by which the file is known to the system. It may be from three to seven characters in length; these may consist of A through Z and 0 through 9. The first character must be alphabetic. If this operand is omitted, the SYS number (SYSnnn) becomes the file's external name.

The RESERVE clause is treated as documentation.

The ORGANIZATION clause specifies the logical structure of the file. When an RRDS is being referenced, a value of RELATIVE must be coded.

Three options are available for the ACCESS MODE clause:

1) SEQUENTIAL
2) RANDOM
3) DYNAMIC

Look at the RELATIVE KEY clause coded in our format example. If SEQUENTIAL access is specified, the RELATIVE KEY clause is optional. However, when RANDOM or DYNAMIC access is chosen, the RELATIVE KEY clause is required.

Just as its name implies, the RELATIVE KEY clause contains the relative record number for a specific record within an RRDS. The data-name is a field defined in the Working-Storage Section; unlike the data-name referenced in a KSDS RECORD KEY clause, the RELATIVE KEY field is not part of the record. Furthermore, the RELATIVE KEY field must be defined as an unsigned integer item.

Why do you ever need to include the RELATIVE KEY clause when sequential access is used?

Sequential access involves reading one record right after another. To reach the one-hundredth record on file, you must first read the 99 records that come before it. True? Yes, unless you use the START statement. In Chapter 2, we first introduced the idea of the START statement. Like a KSDS, an RRDS will also support this particular statement.

If you use a START statement, a RELATIVE KEY clause is required even though sequential access is used. This clause communicates to the START statement where access is to begin. Although you may include the RELATIVE KEY clause anytime sequential access is used, it's ignored unless a START statement is issued.

On the other hand, when random or dynamic access is chosen, the RELATIVE KEY clause is required. How else could you communicate to the computer the relative record number to be accessed?

The PASSWORD clause is optional for an RRDS. If coded, the data-name specified in a PASSWORD clause must be defined in the Working-Storage Section as an alphanumeric item. The first eight characters of this field are used as the password; a shorter field is padded with blanks to eight characters. The password must be equivalent to the one that is defined through the appropriate AMS utility when an RRDS is established.

VSAM enables you to restrict access to some or all of your files. Password-protected files cannot be opened unless valid passwords are supplied; that's why we have the option of including a PASSWORD clause. More about this security feature in Chapter 10.

The FILE STATUS clause operates the same as it does for the other two types of VSAM files. Whenever an I/O statement is executed, a code is placed in the FILE STATUS field. The latter can then be checked through program logic to determine whether the I/O operation was successfully executed.

The data-name specified in a FILE STATUS clause must be defined in the Working-Storage Section as a two-character alphanumeric item. It must not be defined in the File Section.

```
FILE-CONTROL.
    SELECT INV-MASTER
        ASSIGN TO SYS010-DA-3340-INVMST
        ORGANIZATION IS RELATIVE
        ACCESS IS SEQUENTIAL
        RELATIVE KEY IS WS-ITEM-NBR
        PASSWORD IS WS-INV-PASSWORD
        FILE STATUS IS INV-STATUS-CODE.
DATA DIVISION.
FILE SECTION.
.
.
.
WORKING-STORAGE SECTION.
01    WS-ITEM-NBR            PIC 9(6)    VALUE ZEROS.
01    WS-INV-PASSWORD        PIC X(8)    VALUE 'INVMST09'.
01    INV-STATUS-CODE        PIC XX.
.
.
.
PROCEDURE DIVISION.
010-OPEN-FILES.
        OPEN INPUT INV-MASTER.
        IF INV-STATUS-CODE NOT EQUAL 00
            GO TO 500-DISPLAY-MESSAGES.
```

In this example are included the RELATIVE KEY, PASSWORD and FILE STATUS clauses. Note that all corresponding data-names are also defined.

By including the RELATIVE KEY clause, we are prepared for a START statement. Remember how we said that sequential access did not require this particular clause unless the START statement is used?

INV-MASTER has a password with a value of 'INVMST09'. This value will be compared to that contained in the cluster's catalog entry (more about the latter when we discuss AMS) before processing will be allowed. If it does not match, a FILE STATUS code of 91 will be issued.

By referencing the INV-STATUS-CODE field, we can determine whether or not I/O operations are successfully executed for INV-MASTER.

Data Division

The following illustrates both requirements and options for the Data Division when an RRDS is referenced:

FILE SECTION.
FD file-name

$$\left[\text{BLOCK CONTAINS [integer TO] integer} \begin{Bmatrix} \text{CHARACTERS} \\ \text{RECORDS} \end{Bmatrix}\right]$$

[RECORD CONTAINS [integer TO] integer CHARACTERS]

$$\text{LABEL} \begin{Bmatrix} \text{RECORD is} \\ \text{RECORDS ARE} \end{Bmatrix} \begin{Bmatrix} \text{STANDARD} \\ \text{OMITTED} \end{Bmatrix}$$

$$\left[\text{VALUE OF system-name is} \begin{Bmatrix} \text{data-name} \\ \text{literal} \end{Bmatrix}\right]$$

$$\left[\text{DATA} \begin{Bmatrix} \text{RECORD is} \\ \text{RECORDS are} \end{Bmatrix} \text{data-name} \quad \text{[data-name] ...]} \quad . \right.$$

Again, I want to emphasize that our goal isn't to teach you COBOL but rather to relate it to VSAM. Each of the three VSAM structures—KSDS, ESDS and RRDS—has unique ways of influencing the language. They also share many common characteristics. For example, an FD for all three structures is coded the same. The following rules always apply:

1) The LABEL RECORD clause is treated as documentation. Although its presence is required, it does not matter whether the STANDARD or OMITTED option is coded.

2) The RECORDING MODE clause must be omitted. Note that our example did not include this particular clause.

3) Although the BLOCK CONTAINS, DATA RECORDS and VALUE OF clauses may be included, the COBOL compiler treats them as documentation only.

Procedure Division

Access methods and I/O statements naturally have a direct relationship with one another. Why? Because I/O statements are how we access records via programs.

In the next several pages, I will illustrate how the following COBOL verbs are used when an RRDS is referenced:

1) OPEN
2) CLOSE
3) READ
4) WRITE
5) REWRITE
6) DELETE

Before elaborating on each of the above, I again want to stress the importance of getting into the habit of using FILE STATUS codes. Check the value of this field each time an I/O operation occurs. Otherwise, it's unpredictable what may be happening during program execution!

$$\text{OPEN} \begin{cases} \text{INPUT file-name [file-name] . . .} \\ \text{OUTPUT file-name [file-name] . . .} \\ \text{I/O file-name [file-name] . . .} \end{cases}$$

Multiple files may be referenced in an OPEN statement. Access methods can be mixed; for example, you can open a SAM file and a VSAM file at the same time.

OPEN PRINT-FILE INV-MASTER.

If the SELECT statement for the RRDS contains a PASS-WORD clause, the field referenced by this clause must contain the valid password for the cluster being referenced; otherwise, the OPEN statement cannot be successfully executed.

When an OPEN INPUT or OPEN I-O statement is executed, the current record pointer is set to the first record physically present on the RRDS. In other words, it is moved to the first occupied slot. If all the slots are empty, the first READ statement will result in an AT END (end-of-file) condition.

The OPEN OUTPUT statement allows you to initially build an RRDS.

In the other VSAM structures—KSDS and ESDS—the OPEN EXTEND option was available. However, the RRDS structure does not support the EXTEND option.

```
CLOSE   file-name   [WITH LOCK]
        [file-name  [WITH LOCK] ] . . .
```

More than one file may be referenced with a CLOSE statement and access methods can be mixed. For example, both SAM and VSAM files can be referenced with the same CLOSE statement:

```
CLOSE  PRINT-FILE
       INV-MASTER.
```

There is only one option available when referencing VSAM files—LOCK. When the LOCK option is used, the file cannot be opened again during the current execution of the program.

The START and INVALID KEY statements were introduced in Chapter 2. I discussed how these statements work together to allow you to begin a sequential read at a specific location in a KSDS.

The RRDS structure also supports usage of the START statement. Always remember that, in some ways, relative keys resemble record keys. The major characteristic shared by both is their ability to allow you direct access to a specific record. That's the reason why both the KSDS and RRDS structures support the START statement. With the START statement, you can logically position at a specific location within an RRDS.

```
START file-name [KEY IS ⎧ EQUAL TO      ⎫ data-name]
                        ⎨ GREATER THAN   ⎬
                        ⎩ NOT LESS THAN  ⎭
```

Did you notice that the above omits an INVALID KEY statement? This statement should not be used if an RRDS is being accessed sequentially. If ACCESS MODE SEQUENTIAL is specified, the INVALID KEY statement should be omitted.

Check the success of your START statement with a FILE STATUS test:

```
MOVE 92086 to WS-ITEM-NBR.
START INV-MASTER
    KEY IS GREATER THAN WS-ITEM-NBR.
IF INV-STATUS-CODE NOT EQUAL 00
    GO TO 500-DISPLAY-MESSAGE.
```

What about other access modes?

Although random and dynamic modes for the RRDS allow you to follow an I/O operation with an INVALID KEY statement, we don't recommend it. Use the FILE STATUS clause instead.

```
FILE-CONTROL.
    SELECT INV-MASTER
        ASSIGN TO SYS010-DA-3340-INVMST
        ORGANIZATION IS RELATIVE
        ACCESS IS SEQUENTIAL
        RELATIVE KEY IS WS-ITEM-NBR
        FILE STATUS IS INV-STATUS-CODE.
DATA DIVISION.
FILE SECTION.
.
.
.

WORKING-STORAGE SECTION.
01   WS-ITEM-NBR              PIC 9(6).
01   INV-STATUS-CODE          PIC XX.
.
.
.

PROCEDURE DIVISION.
010-OPEN-FILES.
    OPEN INPUT INV-MASTER.
    IF INV-STATUS-CODE NOT EQUAL 00
```

```
        GO TO 500-DISPLAY-MESSAGE.
020-START-RTN.
    MOVE 102354 TO WS-ITEM-NBR.
    START INV-MASTER
        KEY IS EQUAL WS-ITEM-NBR.
```

Note that SEQUENTIAL access has been specified. The RELATIVE KEY is contained in a field called WS-ITEM-NBR. INV-MASTER has been opened as an INPUT file. By the way, the START statement may only be used if a file is opened as INPUT or I-O.

Using the START statement, we will position ourselves at the logical record housed in slot 102354. The latter is also referred to as the record's relative record number. Starting with this particular record, subsequent READ statements will sequentially retrieve records from the RRDS until an end-of-file condition or another START statement is encountered.

SEQUENTIAL RETRIEVAL
    READ file-name   [NEXT] RECORD   [INTO identifier]
[AT END imperative-statement]

RANDOM RETRIEVAL
    READ file-name RECORD   [INTO identifier]
[INVALID KEY imperative-statement]

There are two formats available for READ statements referencing an RRDS. When the sequential format is used, the READ statement makes available the next logical record on file. The random format makes available a specific record; that's why we have the RELATIVE KEY clause.

When you specify (or let it default to) ACCESS MODE SEQUENTIAL for an RRDS, all READ statements must adhere to the sequential format. ACCESS MODE RANDOM requires the random format.

The DYNAMIC mode, however, comes with a slightly more involved set of rules:

1) Either sequential or random record retrieval may be specified.

2 If the sequential format is used, the NEXT option must be included.

3) When records are to be randomly retrieved, the random format must be used.

```
READ INV-MASTER.
IF INV-STATUS-CODE NOT EQUAL 00
    GO TO 500-DISPLAY-MESSAGE.
```

This is an example of the sequential format. Records will be sequentially retrieved in ascending sequence according to slot number.

```
FILE-CONTROL.
    SELECT INV-MASTER
        ASSIGN TO SYS010-DA-3340-INVMST
        ORGANIZATION IS RELATIVE
        ACCESS IS RANDOM
        RELATIVE KEY IS WS-ITEM-NBR
        FILE STATUS IS INV-STATUS-CODE.
.
.
.
PROCEDURE DIVISION.
.
.
.
    SUBTRACT 100000 FROM WS-ITEM-NBR.
    READ INV-MASTER.
```

Notice anything unusual about the RELATIVE KEY field? We subtracted 100000 from WS-ITEM-NBR prior to issuing the READ statement. What this means is that you can actually compute the relative key. Frankly, it doesn't matter how the value of this field originates. The only condition is that it should contain a valid value whenever random retrieval is to be used.

WRITE record-name [FROM identifier]
    [INVALID KEY imperative-statement]

The WRITE statement releases a logical record to a file which has been opened as OUTPUT or I-O.

Now, let's take a look at how ACCESS MODE affects the WRITE operation. When an OUTPUT file is involved, the following actions occur:

1) ACCESS MODE SEQUENTIAL—The first record written to the RRDS has a relative record number of 1. Slots for subsequent records are incremented by 1; thus, the second record released goes to slot number 2, the third to slot number 3, etc.

2) ACCESS MODE RANDOM or DYNAMIC—The RELATIVE KEY field must contain the desired relative record number before a WRITE statement is issued. This number specifies the slot number to be used for your new record.

A file opened as I/O also has some unique rules:

1) You must specify either RANDOM or DYNAMIC access.

2) The RELATIVE KEY field must contain the desired relative record number before a WRITE statement is issued. The value of this field indicates the slot number where the record is to be inserted.

REWRITE record-name [FROM identifier]
[INVALID KEY imperative-statement]

The REWRITE statement allows you to logically modify an existing record. In the case of an Inventory System, perhaps you want to change the vendor name, date last ordered, quantity in stock, etc. Anytime you're using a REWRITE statement (regardless of which VSAM structure is involved), keep in mind the following:

1) The associated file must be opened as I-O.

2) The length of both the new record and the one being replaced must be the same. You cannot reduce or expand the record size.

How do you tell VSAM which logical record in the RRDS is to be changed?

Use the RELATIVE RECORD key if you've chosen direct access. When ACCESS MODE RANDOM or DYNAMIC is specified, the data item defined as the relative key field must contain the relative record number for the record you wish to REWRITE.

When ACCESS MODE SEQUENTIAL is specified, the record to be modified is the one obtained by the last executed READ statement.

```
REWRITE INV-MASTER-REC.
IF INV-STATUS-CODE NOT EQUAL 00
    PERFORM . . .
```

That's all you need if ACCESS MODE SEQUENTIAL is specified in the file's SELECT statement. Did you notice that there is no reference to the RELATIVE KEY FIELD? That's because we're reading the RRDS sequentially, one record slot at a time.

```
MOVE 110921 TO WS-ITEM-NBR.
REWRITE INV-MASTER-REC.
IF INV-STATUS-CODE NOT EQUAL 00
    PERFORM . . .
```

This time, we don't even need a READ statement for the record being referenced. Why? Because an access mode of RANDOM or DYNAMIC has been specified. Look how we used the RELATIVE KEY field. We're going to modify the record housed in slot number 110921.

DELETE file-name RECORD
    [INVALID KEY imperative-statement]

Just as its name implies, the DELETE statement is used to logically remove records from an RRDS. Before record(s) can be removed, however, first the associated file must be opened as I-O.

If ACCESS MODE SEQUENTIAL has been specified, you first need a successfully executed READ statement before a record can be deleted. In other words, the record deleted is the last one read. Also, remember not to follow the DELETE with an INVALID KEY statement if sequential access is used. Check the FILE STATUS code.

Random and dynamic access references the RELATIVE KEY field to determine the record to be deleted. By loading this field with the slot number of the record you wish to remove from the RRDS, you can do just that without ever issuing a READ statement for the file.

```
MOVE 120647 TO WS-ITEM-NBR.
DELETE INV-MASTER.
```

Here, relative record number 120647 will be deleted from INV-MASTER.

Once a DELETE statement is successfully executed, the record is logically gone. Your program can no longer access it. The physical space once occupied by this record can be used again.

There is one restriction, though. Any new record occupying the physical area used by a previously deleted record must be referenced by the same relative record number. Why? Because it now occupies that slot, and as we said at the beginning of this chapter, slots and relative record numbers are the main design components of an RRDS.

5
CHAPTER

The JCL
Connection

Anytime you want to execute a program, JCL is a "must." JCL
(Job Control Language) is what connects software and hardware. As programmers, we can define many different file
descriptions in our programs. We can open VSAM files, printers
and card readers. We can develop coding to write files on
magnetic tape reels. We can reference DAM, SAM, and VSAM
files in the same program.

However, what good is a program unless you can execute
it?

If you don't regard a program listing as fine art to be hung
on walls, then execution is the goal! JCL statements help make
program execution possible. Through special formats and
keywords, files housed on different physical devices may be
referenced by software logic.

What I specifically want to show you in this chapter is how
VSAM affects JCL statements. Not only do access methods
influence program code, but they also affect the physical devices
associated with programs.

Before we get into the nitty-gritty details of JCL coding for
VSAM files, let's talk about *catalogs*. (No, not core image libraries
and phases.)

The concept of catalogs is a core component in the physical
design of DASD storage for VSAM files. Catalogs help mark the
physical location of VSAM files so much that JCL statements

referencing them must identify the catalogs housing such files.

A VSAM data set needs data space. What I mean by "data space" is the physical space on DASD. DOS supports two different types of file storage:

1) Suballocatable data space—stores multiple data sets in an existing VSAM data space.

2) Unique data set—defined in its own data space so that no other file can be stored in that space.

The catalog helps VSAM keep track of the data space it owns and the data sets that occupy it. When you order merchandise by mail, you typically get a catalog first and review it. The catalog gives you a description of the articles for sale as well as such related data as prices and shipping costs.

The VSAM catalog acts in a similar fashion. All the descriptive information needed by VSAM regarding data space and data sets is contained in the VSAM catalog. Examples of such information are CI size, free space percentage, data set name, device type, etc.

When AMS utilities are used to define data space for a file, this is commonly referred to as a "file being cataloged." Another way to describe what happens is to say that a file definition is an "entry to a catalog."

All VSAM files must be cataloged. There are two types of catalogs: *master* and *user*. Each installation has only one master catalog, which is identified to the operating system at IPL time. It is always contained on a DASD volume named SYSCAT. Your systems programmer will place in the standard label area supporting DLBL and EXTENT statements for the file-ID and volume of the master catalog. The filename for the master catalog must be IJSYSCT.

Of course, if your data center is running three independent computers, then you could have three master catalogs. When it comes to user catalogs, however, you may have as many as you like. It is wise, though, to establish some standards in an effort to keep control over the creation of user catalogs. Don't run a "free-for-all" show; sooner or later, you'll pay in confusion or, worse yet, inadequate backup.

In Fig. 5-1, the master catalog points to file and volume entries as well as two user catalogs. Remember that none or any number of user catalogs may exist. Note that, like the master catalog, each user catalog also points to file and volume entries.

Did you notice that the entries for our two user catalogs differ?

VSAM files aren't the exclusive users of catalogs: For example, data space may also be defined for SAM files.

The master catalog always contains a pointer to each user catalog. With the exception of this pointer, a user catalog contains the same kind of information as the master. Furthermore, a non-VSAM data set (such as a SAM file) can be cataloged in either type of catalog.

How do catalogs benefit programmers?

First, they provide us with an excellent means to monitor data space usage. By running special AMS utilities, we can analyze how well or how poorly our VSAM files are functioning.

Secondly, they help to simplify our coding requirements. Much of the required information for processing data is contained in the catalog. Therefore, you don't have to specify it in your applications program. We'll talk more about what's involved in defining catalogs while discussing the DEFINE CLUSTER command in Chapter 7.

Most data centers require that all data sets be defined in user catalogs versus a master catalog. User catalogs can improve VSAM reliability and improve system performance. For example, if the user catalog becomes inoperative, you can still process data sets defined in other user catalogs. Also, by spreading data set information over several catalogs, the time required to locate information is reduced.

Now, let's say a DASD unit fails and the catalog is destroyed. Is everything lost? No. Only the information connected with the catalog housed on the failed DASD unit is lost; only this information needs to be reconstructed. (Just think how much information we're talking about if the master catalog is the only one in your data center: To quote a famous old saying, "It's not always wise to put all of your eggs in one basket.")

Catalogs may also be defined with a *recoverable attribute*. This enables VSAM to record the information about a specific

VSAM CATALOG RELATIONSHIPS

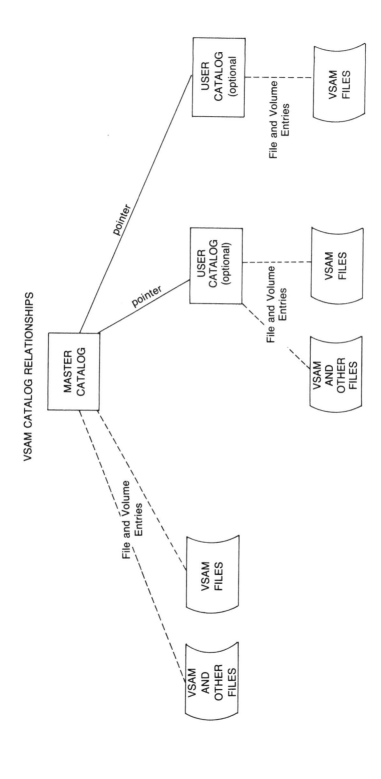

FIG. 5-1. VSAM Catalog Relationships

73

volume and its files in two places—the volume and the catalog itself. If for any reason the catalog is destroyed, you can reconstruct it by using the duplicate information recorded on the volume(s) that it owns.

JCL REQUIREMENTS

VSAM actually made JCL coding easier for applications programmers. EXTENT statements are no longer needed. The VSAM catalog contains all information dealing with DASD allocations.

To show you how easy it is to write DOS JCL for VSAM files, I've taken an excerpt from a COBOL program (INV999) and included its accompanying JCL.

The File Select Clauses

```
SELECT INV-MASTER
    ASSIGN SYS010-DA-3340-INVMST
    ORGANIZATION IS INDEXED
    ACCESS IS RANDOM
    RECORD KEY IS INV-ITEM-NBR
    FILE STATUS IS INV-STATUS-CODE.
SELECT PRINT-FILE
    ASSIGN SYS011-UR-3203-S.
```

The JCL

```
// JOB INV999
// ASSGN SYS011,SYSLST
// DLBL INVMST,'INV.MASTER.FILE', ,VSAM
// EXEC INV999,SIZE = AUTO
/*
/&
```

Other access methods using DASD files require ASSGN and EXTENT statements for each file. VSAM files, however, need only a DLBL statement. (However, if you follow my recommendation and develop user catalogs, an additional DLBL statement will be needed. More about this shortly.)

As you can see, our sample DLBL statement is comprised of three parameters that represent minimal coding requirements for a VSAM file. By the way, have you noticed that not once have I referred to VSAM structures? When it comes to JCL, it doesn't make any difference whether you're dealing with a KSDS, ESDS or RRDS.

Now for a review of each DLBL parameter included in our example:

1) *filename*—INVMST is the filename. Note in the COBOL excerpt that an external filename was associated with the file. Therefore, we must reference INVMST in the JCL rather than SYS010.

2) *file-ID*—'INV.MASTER.FILE'.

3) *code*—VSAM.

The idea of clusters was introduced earlier in this book. Clusters, also referred to as file entries, are defined to VSAM catalogs using AMS utilities. (I'll tell you how to do this in Chapter 7.) For now, what I want to emphasize is that the filename specified on the DLBL statement must agree with the cluster name. In other words, 'INV.MASTER.FILE' was defined to a VSAM catalog as cluster INVMST.

VSAM-related JCL for application programs is obviously simple. However, don't forget that continuation cards are supported for DLBL statements. To accomplish this, column 72 must contain a continuation character (usually a C); the columns between the last comma and this continuation character must be blanks, and the continuation card must start in column 16.

```
// DLBL filename,'file-ID', ,VSAM [,BUFSP = n]
          [,CAT = catalog-name][,DISP = disp]
```

This format is valid for VSAM files only. Format differences exist when other access methods are used. A comma must be inserted for each positional operand that is omitted if any of the subsequent operands are used.

filename	May consist of from one to seven alphanumeric characters. The first character must be alphabetic. VSAM requires the *filename* parameter to agree with the related external filename housed in the executing program's SELECT statement. This name must also agree with the filename specified when IDCAMS is used to define the cluster.
file-ID	May consist of from one to 44 alphanumeric characters. The file-ID's first character must be alphabetic or notational (A-Z, @, $, #).
VSAM	Indicative of the access method being used.
BUFSP = n	Specifies the number of bytes allocated for buffer space. This allocation is in terms of virtual storage. "n" can range from 0 to 999999. BUFSP is an optional parameter. If present, however, it overrides the buffer space allocation designated by previous IDCAMS control statements.
CAT =	Contains the name of a VSAM catalog. This catalog name consists of from one to seven characters. The specified catalog must own the VSAM file being referenced through your DLBL's file-ID parameter. Code this parameter only if you need to override the computer's assumption that the job catalog owns the file or, if there is no job catalog, that the master catalog owns the file.
DISP =	May be specified only for a reusable file when it is opened and closed. A reusable VSAM file is one that can be reused for work files regardless of its contents. Valid values for this parameter are:

```
NEW
(NEW,KEEP)
(NEW,DELETE)
(NEW,DATE)
OLD
(OLD,KEEP)
(OLD,DELETE)
(OLD,DATE)
```

(,KEEP)
(,DELETE)
(,DATE)

NEW	Specifies that the file is to be reset at open.
OLD	Specifies that the file is not to be reset at open.
,KEEP	Specifies that the file is to be kept at close.
,DELETE	Specifies that the file's contents is to be made inaccessible at close.
DATE	Specifies that the disposition is the same as for KEEP (if the expiration date has not been reached) or DELETE (if the expiration date has been reached).

The DISP parameter is generally not coded because most VSAM files aren't reusable. Since most application programmers will never have a need for this type of VSAM file, I chose not to include much discussion about them in this book. For an in-depth explanation, refer to the IBM manuals listed in the Bibliography.

If you do have a reusable file but omit the DISP parameter, DOS will use (OLD,KEEP) by default. Thus, no data is lost.

JOB CATALOGS

I recommend that all VSAM data sets be defined in user catalogs rather than the master catalog. If your data center adopts this standard, a *job catalog* can simplify JCL coding requirements.

A job catalog is a way of identifying to VSAM the user catalog that is to be referenced for a job. This catalog is created by using the filename IJSYSUC in the DLBL statement that specifies the user catalog:

// DLBL IJSYSUC,'INV.USER.CATALOG',,VSAM,CAT = IJSYSCT

Unless you specify otherwise, DOS assumes that all subsequent DLBL statements for VSAM files refer to files cataloged in the user catalog identified by the DLBL IJSYSUC statement. In our example, the user catalog is INV.USER.CATALOG. When DLBL statements are coded for VSAM files contained in this user catalog, the CAT parameter may be coded as CAT = IJSYSUC. However, it may also be omitted since DOS uses IJSYSUC by default.

If you wish to access a file owned by a catalog other than the job catalog, you must code the CAT parameter on its DLBL statement. Furthermore, the job stream must include a DLBL statement for the other user catalog; here, filename other than IJSYSUC is required. The filename coded on the user catalog's DLBL statement must agree with the value coded for the CAT parameter on DLBLs for files owned by this other user catalog.

```
/ / JOB INV500
/ / DLBL IJSYSUC,'INV.USER.CATALOG', ,VSAM,CAT = IJSYSCT
/ / DLBL INVMST,'INV.MASTER.FILE', ,VSAM
/ / DLBL INVCTL,'INV.CONTROL.LOG', ,VSAM
/ / DLBL INVTRN,'INV.TRANSACTIONS', ,VSAM
/ / DLBL GLCAT,'GL.USER.CATALOG', ,VSAM,CAT = IJSYSCT
/ / DLBL GLTRNS,'GL.TRAN.FILE', ,VSAM,CAT = GLCAT
/ / EXEC INV500,SIZE = AUTO
/*
/&
```

In this example, two user catalogs are referenced. INV.MASTER.FILE, INV.CONTROL.LOG, and INV.TRANSACTIONS are owned by the job catalog. Thus, the CAT parameter may be omitted. The GL.TRAN.FILE is owned by a different user catalog which has a filename of GLCAT. The name GLCAT appears on both the DLBL statement identifying the catalog as well as the CAT parameter for the file owned by this particular catalog.

Job catalogs are not required. If you so desire, you may specify each user catalog to be referenced as for GL.USER.CATALOG. As you can clearly see from the example, job catalogs reduce coding requirements.

HIERARCHY OF CATALOG CONTROL

Catalogs are searched for VSAM file entries in the following order:

1) *Explicit user* or *master catalog.* Specified by the AMS CATALOG parameter or by the CAT = parameter on a DLBL statement.

2) *Job catalog.* If the above catalog is not specified, the job catalog is searched. This catalog is specified on a DLBL statement coded with a filename of IJSYSUC.

3) *Master catalog.* If none of the above catalogs are specified, the master catalog (IJSYSCT) is searched.

•

In the summary of job catalogs above, you discovered that references to catalogs require additional JCL statements.

All application programs must specify a DLBL statement for the master catalog unless a DLBL and EXTENT for it is placed in the partition or standard label area. I strongly urge that your data center use the partition or standard label area; what a great way to save JCL coding time!

If the program is accessing a file defined in a user catalog, you must supply one of the following:

1) A job catalog DLBL (IJSYSUC) statement for that user catalog.

2) A DLBL statement for the user catalog. Each file referenced by the program and contained in this user catalog must have its DLBL statement coded with the CAT = parameter. The latter must then reference the filename given in the user catalog's DLBL statement.

In all situations, both ASSGN and EXTENT statements are optional:

/ / EXEC phase-name,SIZE = xxx

Before I discuss the parameters comprising an EXEC statement for programs referencing VSAM files, I want to emphasize one very important fact. I omitted the REAL parameter because it cannot be specified for programs using VSAM or ISAM running under the IIP.

The SIZE parameter, however, must always be specified for either of the above. It specifies how many K bytes of storage are to be used for the program when it's executed in virtual storage. If you don't know how much storage to request, you can code SIZE = AUTO and DOS will automatically calculate the proper amount. The only exception to this rule is when the COBOL program contains a SORT statement. When the latter is present, one available option is to code SIZE = (AUTO,nK). "n" is a minimum of 16; DOS automatically adds the K amount onto the value it calculates.

Now, let's take another look at the EXEC statement along with a brief explanation of its parameters.

/ / EXEC phase-name,SIZE = xxx

Phase-name Indicates the phase to be executed. This phase must be cataloged to a core image library.

SIZE xxx Specifies how much storage is needed for loading the phase into memory. Any of the following formats are supported:

1) Where xxx is n, there must be a minimum of 16. Also, it should be a multiple of 2.

2) Where xxx is AUTO, the program size will be calculated by the system from information contained in the core image directory. This is the easiest format to use.

3) Where xxx is (AUTO, nK), the program size plus nK bytes will be used as the value for SIZE. n should be a multiple of 2.

A certain amount of storage is required anytime you execute a program that references VSAM files. It uses more storage than other access methods because it needs storage to allocate its I/O buffers and control blocks. Forty-K is needed for a catalog, 12K for a KSDS, and 10K for an RRDS or ESDS. Naturally, the more VSAM files you have, the more storage you'll need. VSAM acquires this storage from the GETVIS area.

6
CHAPTER

The Access Method Services Program

Isn't it easier to say AMS, rather than Access Method Services program? Although it's short and easy to say, you could nevertheless describe it as the "heart of VSAM." It is an important utility and service program. Just like your heart is the core of your existence, AMS supports the VSAM environment. Having at least a basic understanding of this sophisticated and multifunctional piece of software is a necessity for anyone who works with VSAM.

Some of the reasons we use AMS are to:

- Define master and user catalogs
- Define DASD space to VSAM
- Define VSAM files
- Load records into a VSAM file from a SAM or ISAM file
- Print a VSAM file
- Create a backup copy of a file
- Delete VSAM files, space and catalogs
- List the VSAM catalog
- Reorganize VSAM files
- Recover from certain types of damage to a file
- Make a file portable from one operating system to another

Now, how do you use AMS?

/ / EXEC IDCAMS,SIZE = AUTO

First, look at the EXEC statement needed to invoke the AMS program. The phase name is IDCAMS. Perhaps you noticed in other chapters how at times I referred to AMS and then on other occasions to IDCAMS.

IDCAMS is the main utility program for processing VSAM files. It is called the Access Method Services program because it can perform a variety of utility services using several different access methods. One example is that it can convert an ISAM file to a VSAM file.

Like most programs, IDCAMS expects input. Along with the tape or DASD files to be processed, it expects a card-image input file. The latter is a set of control statements called *commands*. These commands instruct the AMS program as to what type of operations should occur. You, the programmer, use these commands to specify which utility functions are needed.

Remember that in the Introduction I said that AMS is practically a language in itself? Well, it is. It's a language of keywords and structural commands.

There are two types of AMS commands:

1) *Functional* to request the actual work (i.e., defining a catalog, printing a VSAM file).

2) *Modal* to specify options and to allow the conditional execution of the functional commands.

There are numerous AMS commands, many of which you, as an applications programmer, will never need. Rather than include all of them and confuse you (or, worse yet, frighten you!), I've elected to discuss only the more popular ones. In this chapter, I will introduce several of these commands, classifying them as functional or modal. In Chapter 7, I'll provide a more detailed explanation of how to use several of the more popular commands.

On more than one occasion, I've compared AMS to a language. In keeping with this analogy, it only makes good sense that AMS has a unique syntax:

command parameters terminator

The *command* specifies the type of operation requested. Some people refer to it as a "verb." *Parameters* further describe the operation. An example of the latter is the record key length for a KSDS. Finally, as its name signifies, the *terminator* ends the command.

Many commands and parameters can be abbreviated. It's quicker to code

DEF AIX

instead of

DEFINE ALTERNATEINDEX

Actually, the term *parameter* is a little vague. A parameter can be either a *positional parameter* or a *keyword parameter*. Together, these parameters are referred to as the command's *parameter set*.

Let's take a look at a positional parameter. As the word "positional" implies, such parameters are characterized by their positions in relation to other parameters. A positional parameter cannot be omitted.

entry-name is a positional parameter for the ALTER command.

ALTER entry-name [/password]
    [CATALOG(name[/password])]
      .
      .
      .
      .

In our example, "entry-name" must be coded, and it must be the first parameter following the ALTER command:

ALTER INVMST[/INV11091]

This command will alter the INVMST data set. The password is INV11091.

TOKEY(92086)

This is an example of a keyword parameter. It's used to indicate a value and is preceded by a specific character string.

TOKEY is the keyword; the value of this parameter is 92086.

A keyword parameter may also have a set of subparameters. An example of this is:

CYLINDERS(primary [secondary])

This specifies the initial space allocation as well as the secondary allocation; "secondary" is a subparameter.

General coding rules for AMS command statements are:

1) IDCAMS control statements follow the EXEC statement.

2) All control statements are coded in 80-column card format. Column 1 should always be blank. Positions 2-72 are used for the command and related parameters, while positions 73-80 may be used for optional identification (i.e., job name) or sequence numbers.

3) Control statements always follow this general pattern:

command parameters terminator

Only one command may be coded per physical record.

4) Names (i.e., clusters) contain one to 44 characters. These characters may be A-Z, 0-9, @, #, $, - (the hyphen) and the 12/0 overpunch (hex CO). Names containing more than eight characters must be separated by a period; between each period, one to eight characters may be coded.

INV.MASTER.FILE

The first character of a name must be A-Z, @, # or $.

5) Positional parameters must always appear first in a parameter set.

6) Keyword parameters always follow related positional parameters. The order of keyword parameters is not fixed.

7) Commands and parameters are separated from each other by one or more blanks, commas or comments.

8) Parameters and subparameters must be separated by a space, comma or comment. There is one exception— parameters immediately preceding or following a subparameter

set enclosed in parentheses do not need to be separated from the opening or closing parentheses.

9) When coding a parameter or a sub-parameter, each is immediately followed by its value. The latter must be enclosed in parentheses unless only one item is specified.

DELETE (INVMST)

is acceptable as well as

DELETE INVMST

10) Statements may be continued. To do so, code a hyphen after a parameter and then begin the next parameter on the following line. You may precede the hyphen with no more than one space, but this is not necessary. Also, no special character is required in any column to indicate a continuation line.

FILE(INV001) -
VOLUME(USER05)

11) Comments may be included anywhere in the IDCAMS input stream. A comment begins with the characters /* and ends with the characters */.

KEY(10)   /*   ITEM NBR   */

Comments may contain any character with the exception of "*/".

12) A plus symbol (+) is used to continue a value in a command.

BLOCKS(102 +
38)
is the same as

BLOCKS(10238)

13) Blank records or records ending with complete comments must end with a continuation symbol (-) if they appear in the middle of a command. Records ending with partial comments must always end with the continuation symbol.

FROMKEY(327)   /*   STARTING POINT   */   -
TOKEY(999)   /*   ENDING POINT   */   -

14) Values cannot contain commas, semicolons, blanks, parentheses or slashes unless the entire value is enclosed in single quotation marks. If you code a single quotation mark in a field enclosed in such symbols, it must be coded as two single quotation marks.

15) A password may appear after the name of the object it is related to. The password is separated from the object's name by a slash (/).

16) The terminator indicates the end of the command. It can be a semicolon (;) or the absence of a continuation symbol. If a semicolon is used, it cannot be enclosed in quotation marks or embedded in a comment. The AMS program will ignore everything to the right of the semicolon.

Now that we've recapped the basic rules for coding AMS statements, a word of warning. Incorrect use of punctuation is an all-too-common reason for a command being considered unacceptable. Other areas prone to user error are continuation characters and parentheses. In other words, if your AMS job stream fails, check out the punctuation very carefully!

•

AMS FUNCTIONAL COMMANDS

Command	Purpose
ALTER	Modifies information specified for a catalog, cluster, alternate index or path at define time.
BLDINDEX	Builds an alternate index.
DEFINE ALTERNATEINDEX	Defines an alternate index.
DEFINE CLUSTER	Defines a VSAM file.
DEFINE MASTERCATALOG	Defines a master catalog.
DEFINE PATH	Defines the path that connects an alternate index to its related cluster.
DEFINE SPACE	Defines DASD space for VSAM usage.
DEFINE USERCATALOG	Defines a user catalog.
DELETE ALTERNATEINDEX	Deletes an alternate index.
DELETE CLUSTER	Deletes a VSAM file.

DELETE MASTERCATALOG	Deletes a master catalog.
DELETE PATH	Deletes the path that connects an alternate index to its related cluster.
DELETE SPACE	Deletes VSAM ownership of DASD space.
DELETE USERCATALOG	Deletes a user catalog.
EXPORT	Creates a copy of a file. This backup is portable so that it may be used in another system (i.e., DOS to MVS conversion).
EXPORTRA	Recovers information independent of catalog status. Duplicate catalog entries are placed in the *catalog recovery areas* (CRAs).
IMPORT	Reads a previously exported file. File may be copied on one system and restored to another (i.e., DOS to MVS conversion).
IMPORTRA	Makes available information recovered via the EXPORTRA command.
LISTCAT	Lists information about catalog entries.
LISTCRA	Lists information about catalog recovery areas. Can also compare entries in the CRA with the appropriate entries in a catalog to check whether the catalog and the CRA are in agreement.
PRINT	Prints the contents of a VSAM or non-VSAM file.
REPRO	Copies records from one file to another. Converts SAM files to VSAM, ISAM files to VSAM, etc. Creates backup copies of VSAM catalogs and reloads VSAM catalogs from such backup copies.

●

AMS MODAL COMMANDS

COMMAND	PURPOSE
IF	Controls the flow-of-command execution. Tests condition codes and follows such tests with THEN and ELSE clauses. The latter specify alternative commands which are executed according to test results.
DO . . . END	Indicates the beginning and ending of a command sequence. These commands usually occur within a THEN and ELSE clause.

SET   Changes condition codes.
PARM   Specifies diagnostic aids. Sets option values which affect AMS execution.

•

More than one functional command may be placed in a job stream, and numerous modal commands may be included with each functional command.

```
/ / JOB VSAM
/ / ASSGN
/ / DLBL
/ / EXTENT
.
.
.
/ / EXEC IDCAMS,SIZE = AUTO
 1   define user catalog
 2   define space
 3   define data set
/*
/&
```

This example illustrates how one job can execute multiple functional commands. Coded this way, AMS will attempt to perform all three functions regardless of whether a preceding command fails. For example, do you really want to execute commands 2 and 3 if command 1 fails? Probably not. That's why I strongly urge you to explore the modal commands. An IF command can be used to prevent execution of a subsequent step if a previous one fails.

Have you noticed that, when discussing modal commands, I include references to condition code testing?

Once a functional command is completed, AMS returns a condition code. These codes are placed in register 15 and indicate whether the request was successfully executed.

0   No errors occurred
4   Some problem was encountered and a warning message
     is issued
8   A command was completed but major related tasks were
     bypassed
12   The command was not performed because of a logical error
16   A severe error occurred causing subsequent commands
     to be ignored

These condition codes can then be referenced through the
modal commands (i.e., IF).

```
IF {LASTCC | MAXCC} relational-operator number
     THEN [command |
          DO
          command-set
          END]
     [ELSE [command |
          DO
          command-set
          END] ]
```

LASTCC	A variable containing the condition code set by the previous AMS command.
MAXCC	A variable containing the highest condition code set by any previous AMS command.
relational-operator	May also be called the *comparand*. Valid values are:
	EQ or = equal to
	NE ≠ not equal to
	GT or > greater than
	LT or < less than
	GE ≥ greater than or equal to
	LE ≤ less than or equal to
number	The decimal value to which LASTCC or MAXCC is compared. Any value over 16 is assumed to be 16.

DOS VSAM for Application Programmers

THEN	Specifies what action is to occur if the test condition is true. Such action may take the form of one or more AMS commands. You may follow THEN with another IF statement.
ELSE	Specifies what action is to occur if the test condition is false. Such action may take the form of one or more AMS commands. You may follow ELSE with another statement.
command	An AMS command.
command-set	One or more AMS commands preceded by the word DO and followed by the word END.

```
IF LASTCC = 0 -
   THEN REPRO INFILE(INV01) OUTFILE(INV02)
   ELSE PRINT . . .
```

Our example says that if the last executed AMS command resulted in a condition code of 0, then a REPRO command will be issued; otherwise, a PRINT command is to be executed.

```
IF MAXCC = 4 THEN
   ELSE DELETE . . .
```

Note that in this example of an IF command, we did not follow THEN with any command statements. This is called a *null clause*. If a THEN or ELSE clause is not followed by a command or a continuation character, no action occurs; thus, we have a null clause.

Why have such a feature?

It comes in handy if no action is required. A null ELSE clause can also help balance out the THENs and ELSEs if you're nesting IF statements.

```
SET {LASTCC | MAXCC} = number
```

| LASTCC | A variable containing the condition code set by the previous AMS command. |
| MAXCC | A variable containing the highest condition set by any previous AMS command. |

number   The decimal value to which LASTCC or MAXCC is set. Any value over 16 is assumed to be 16. If 16 is coded or assumed, AMS terminates since such a value represents a severe error condition.

```
SET MAXCC = 12
```

The maximum condition code variable (MAXCC) will be set to 12.

```
IF LASTCC > 0 -
    THEN SET MAXCC = 16
    .
    .
    .
```

This time, we combined IF and SET commands. If the previous AMS command resulted in a condition code greater than 0, the MAXCC variable will be set to 16. Since a value of 16 is used, AMS will automatically terminate.

```
PARM [TEST ({[TRACE]
           [AREAS (areaid [areaid . . . ] ) ]
           [FULL ((dumpid [count1 [count2] ] )
             [ (dumpid . . .] ) ] |
           [OFF] } )
           ]
      [GRAPHICS (CHAIN (chain) | TABLE (mname) ) ]
      [MARGINS (leftmargin rightmargin)]
      [SYNCHK]
```

The PARM command can specify processing options for diagnostic aids as well as the format for the printed output resulting from AMS commands.

The portion of the PARM command that controls diagnostic aids is:

```
TEST ({[TRACE]
    [AREAS (areaid [areaid . . .] ) ]
    FULL ( ( dumpid [count1 [count2] ] )
      [ (dumpid . . .) ] ) ] |
    [off] } )
```

Once the TEST option has been set, it remains in effect until it is reset by another PARM command. The TRACE, AREAS and FULL parameters may be used in the same command statement.

The TRACE parameter requests a listing of trace tables whenever the built-in dump points of the processor are encountered.

The AREAS (areaid . . . parameter identifies which modules are to have selected variables dumped at their dump points. Each *areaid* is a two-character area-identifier defined during AMS implementation. Check with your systems programming staff for specifics pertaining to your data center.

The FULL((dumpid[count1 [count2]]) . . . parameter requests a partition dump as well as the trace tables and selected variables at the specified points. Here, *dumpid* represents a four-character identifier of the dump point, and *count1* is a decimal number that specifies how many times the program is to encounter the dump point before beginning the dump listing. *count2* is a decimal number that specifies the number of encounters at a dump point for which dumps are to be listed. *count1* and *count2* must range between 1 and 32,767; a default value of 1 is assumed.

The OFF parameter stops the use of diagnostic aids.

The GRAPHICS option of the PARM command controls print options for output resulting from AMS commands.

GRAPHICS (CHAIN(chain) | TABLE (mname))

This specifies the print chain/train graphic character set or a special graphics table to be used when output is printed.

CHAIN(chain)   *chain* indicates the graphic character set of the print chain or train. Valid values are AN, HN, PN, QN, RN, SN and TN. The default value is PN.

TABLE(mname)   *mname* is the name of an entry in the core image library that contains a 256-byte user-provided translate table.

The MARGINS option of the PARM command controls the format of input records. Remember that AMS control statements are really just input records to the IDCAMS program.

MARGINS(leftmargin rightmargin)

This specifies where the margins are for input records.

leftmargin   Indicates where the left margin begins. The default value is 2.

rightmargin   Indicates where the right margin begins. The default value is 72.

The SYNCHK option of the PARM command controls syntax-checking. If coded, SYNCHK requests that commands are to be checked for correct syntax but not executed. When execution is desired, this option must be removed.

The PARM command is rarely used by most applications programmers. If you feel you have a need for it, I recommend you discuss this with your systems programming staff prior to issuing the command. Although PARM cannot result in damage to the VSAM program or the operating system, you may be somewhat surprised by the output—especially the dumps—unless you're a whiz at AMS debugging!

AMS MESSAGES

The AMS program does a pretty good job of letting you know what happens when commands are issued. In some cases, messages are displayed on the console for the computer operator to review. The majority of messages, though, are sent to SYSLST. By reviewing this printed output, operators and programmers can determine the success of an IDCAMS job.

Console messages related to AMS commands are prefixed with IDC.

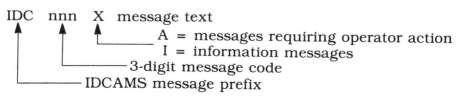

93

Printed messages related to AMS commands are also prefixed with IDC. These messages, however, are followed by four- and five-digit message codes rather than the three-digit code used for console messages. Furthermore, no operator action is associated with printed messages.

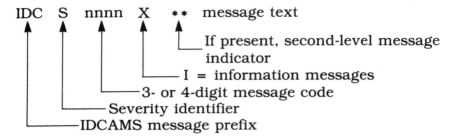

IDC S nnnn X ** message text
                  └─ If present, second-level message indicator
               └──── I = information messages
         └────────── 3- or 4-digit message code
      └───────────── Severity identifier
   └──────────────── IDCAMS message prefix

Valid values for *severity identifier* are:

0   Information only—has no effect on execution
1   Warning—successful execution is very likely
2   Error—execution may fail
3   Serious error—successful execution is unlikely
4   Terminating error—successful execution is impossible

Note that the *severity identifier* and *message code* count is one unit when referencing the message number. That's how we can get a maximum of five digits for a message identifier.

The latter illustration also includes a code signifying that a second-level message is present which further explains the preceding message. Sometimes they're fairly self-explanatory; you can read the message and understand what type of corrective action to take. Their main purpose, though, is to provide you with a reference number.

Get IBM's VSE/VSAM Messages and Codes (SC24-5146) manual. The IDC prefix tells us this is the proper guide to use, since IDC specifies that a VSAM-related error has occurred. The *message number* can then point you to a more detailed explanation of the message.

7
CHAPTER

Using IDCAMS

Like any other program, IDCAMS needs JCL statements to successfully execute. It recognizes both input and output files. In fact, the AMS commands are input files; they're entered in card-image format. Don't forget, though, that the main purpose behind IDCAMS is to manipulate data sets. It allows us to establish user catalogs, create backup copies of files, convert ISAM files to the KSDS structure, etc. So, doesn't it make good sense that there must be some way to assign these files to the program?

In Chapter 5, I first introduced the necessity of JCL statements for catalog assignments. In that chapter, we concentrated on application programs that use VSAM files. Now we will examine the utility program IDCAMS. There are similarities here; DLBL statements are needed for any VSAM files referenced by the AMS job, and such statements must use the VSAM format.

VSAM files referenced by an AMS job must be identified by certain JCL information when an I/O operation is being performed. If, for example, you just want to request a LISTCAT, no JCL statements are needed for the clusters or catalogs involved since this is not an I/O operation.

There are times when you may need to assign tape files. For example, a tape assignment may be needed when the IMPORT command is used. Both unlabeled and standard labeled tapes are supported.

AMS "expects" tape and disk file assignment as follows:

	Input	Output
tape	SYS004	SYS005
disk	SYS006	SYS007

Although SYS006 and SYS007 are the standard assignments for disk files, other SYS numbers may be used. You can accomplish this by coding ASSGN, DLBL and EXTENT statements, maintaining consistency with whatever SYS numbers you choose.

When IDCAMS is executed, an activity report is generated. SYSLST is always used for this output file. However, an ASSGN statement is not necessary.

I have not included in this book an in-depth presentation of the JCL statements necessary to support all AMS commands. As I said earlier, the subject of AMS alone can easily fill an entire text. Furthermore, many AMS functions such as defining master catalogs and setting up the necessary JCL statements are typically handled by systems programmers.

What I hope to provide is a general understanding of the more frequently-used AMS commands. For a detailed example of IDCAMS and its JCL requirements, refer to IBM's DOS/VS Access Method Services User's Guide (GC33-5382). This useful manual will also provide you with an excellent presentation of all available AMS parameters.

Now, let's briefly review three formats for DASD files requiring supporting JCL statements.

/ / ASSGN sysnbr,disk-type,volser,SHR

sysnbr	Identifies the SYS number. SYS006 is generally used for an input file and SYS007 for an output file.
disk-type	Valid values are CKD or FBA.
	CKD is count-key data
	FBA is fixed-block architecture
volser	Identifies the DASD volume being used.
SHR	Specifies that the unit is shareable.

/ / DLBL filename,file-ID,,VSAM

filename   Identifies the file. Must correspond to the *filename*
              (more about this shortly) of an INFILE, OUTFILE,
              WORKFILE or FILE parameter in an AMS com-
              mand.

file-ID   Identical to the name given a file in the catalog
              when the file was defined using the AMS DEFINE
              command. Is identical to the *name, entryname,
              catname* or *newname* parameter in an AMS
              command.

VSAM   Identifies the access method.

/ / EXTENT sysnbr,volser

sysnbr   Identifies the SYS number. Must agree with that
              used in the corresponding ASSGN statement.

volser   Identifies the DASD volume being used. Must
              agree with that used in the corresponding ASSGN
              statement.

Now we're going to explore some of the more frequently-
used AMS commands. In most cases, I have not included all
available parameters, opting instead for just the most common
ones. Also, some popular AMS commands have been excluded
from this particular chapter since they are discussed in later
chapters. One example of this is LISTCAT; it has been included
in Chapter 9 because of the important role it plays in the tuning
process.

DEFINE

Using the AMS DEFINE command, several objects must be
defined before any actual file processing can begin. The
definable objects are:

1) MASTERCATALOG
2) USERCATALOG
3) SPACE
4) CLUSTER
5) ALTERNATEINDEX
6) PATH

97

Everything from catalog characteristics to the physical DASD location of the cluster must be defined. Furthermore, all of these definitions must be accomplished before the actual file can be loaded.

Is it always necessary to define each of these objects before loading a file?

No. The MASTERCATALOG is an excellent example. Once your system programmer defines this catalog and the DASD space associated with it, it's doubtful that you'll need to run any AMS jobs affecting it. Another example is the DEFINE ALTERNATEINDEX command. If you're loading an RRDS, alternate indexes aren't even allowed, so of course you wouldn't need to use the related AMS command.

DEFINE MASTERCATALOG

The DEFINE MASTERCATALOG command (DEF MCAT) is used to establish a VSAM master catalog. Actually, this is the first step towards creating a VSAM system. You do not have to precede this operation with a DEFINE SPACE command; when the master catalog is defined, you are implicitly defining the VSAM space for it.

```
DEFINE MASTERCATALOG
        (NAME(entryname)
        FILE(filename)
        VOLUME(volser)
        {BLOCKS(primary [secondary] ) |
        CYLINDERS(primary [secondary] ) |
        RECORDS(primary [secondary] ) |
        TRACKS(primary [secondary] )}
        [MASTERPW(password)]
        [READPW(password)]
        [UPDATEPW(password)]
        )
```

The following are required parameters:

NAME   The value coded for *entryname* is the name that must be used in all future references to the master catalog. *entryname* may consist of one to 44 characters. These characters may be A-Z, 0-9, @, #, $, - (the hyphen) and the 12/0 overpunch (hex C0.) Names containing more than eight characters must be separated by a period; between each period, one to eight characters may be coded. The first character of an *entryname* must be A-Z, @, # or $.

FILE   Specifies the *filename* coded on the DLBL statement; the latter must be included in the JCL used to execute IDCAMS and the DEFINE MASTER-CATALOG command. For the master catalog, the *filename* must be IJSYSCT.

VOLUME   May be abbreviated as VOL. Specifies the DASD volume that is to contain the master catalog. This volume cannot be owned by any other VSAM catalog.

The following four parameters control allocation of physical space. You may choose whichever option you like best, but one of the four must be selected. Both *primary* and *secondary* allocations can be made. These values may be expressed in decimal, hexadecimal or binary. Values expressed in hexadecimal must be preceded by X; values expressed in binary must be preceded by B. Hexadecimal and binary values must also be enclosed in single quotation marks and cannot be longer than one full word.

BLOCKS   Specifies how many FBA blocks are to be allocated. Supported for FBA devices only.

CYLINDERS   May be abbreviated as CYL. Specifies the number of cylinders to be allocated.

RECORDS   May be abbreviated as REC. Specifies the number of records for which space is to be allocated. Each record contained in a master catalog consists of 512 bytes.

TRACKS   May be abbreviated as TRK. Specifies the number of tracks to be allocated.

The following are three optional parameters that deal with password protection. A *password* may consist of one to eight

EBCDIC characters. If it contains commas, semicolons, blanks, parentheses or slashes, the password must be enclosed in single quotation marks. If you include a single quotation mark within a password, it must be coded as two single quotation marks whenever the password is enclosed in single quotation marks.

Passwords can be expressed in hexadecimal. Two hexadecimal characters represent one EBCDIC character. The hexadecimal value must be preceded by X and enclosed in single quotation marks.

MASTERPW   May be abbreviated as MRPW. Specifies a master level password for the master catalog. If any files connected to the catalog are password protected, a master password must be present. The master password allows all I/O operations.

READPW   May be abbreviated as RDPW. Specifies a read level password for the master catalog. The read password permits read operations only.

UPDATEPW   May be abbreviated as UPDPW. Specifies an update level password for the master catalog. The update password permits both read and write operations.

When you execute IDCAMS for the DEFINE MASTER CATALOG command, certain JCL coding conventions must be followed. The filename coded on the DLBL statement must be IJSYSCT. Use the value coded for the NAME parameter as the DLBL's *file-ID*. The logical unit referenced in the EXTENT statement must be SYSCAT. Information contained in the EXTENT statement must agree with the VOLUME parameter and the CYLINDERS, TRACKS or RECORDS parameter.

```
/ /  JOB MASTCAT
/ /  DLBL IJSYSCAT,'VSAM.MASTER.CATALOG',,VSAM
/ /  EXTENT SYSCAT,SYSRES,1,0,19,6650
/ /  EXEC IDCAMS,SIZE = AUTO
       DEFINE   MASTERCATALOG              -
                (NAME(VSAM.MASTER.CATALOG)  -
                FILE(IJSYSCT)              -
```

```
        VOLUME(SYSRES)                    -
        CYL(350)                          -
        MASTERPW(MCATPW1)                 -
        3UPDATEPW(MCATPW2)                -
/ *
/ &
```

DEFINE USERCATALOG

The DEFINE USERCATALOG command (DEF UCAT) is used to establish a VSAM user catalog. You do not have to precede this operation with a DEFINE SPACE command; when the user catalog is defined, you are implicitly defining the VSAM space for it.

The DASD volume that contains the user catalog must not be owned by any other VSAM catalog. A pointer to the user catalog is automatically placed in the master catalog.

```
DEFINE USERCATALOG
        (NAME(entryname)
        FILE(filename)
        VOLUME(volser)
        {BLOCKS(primary [secondary] ) |
        CYLINDERS(primary [secondary]) |
        RECORDS(primary [secondary] ) |
        TRACKS(primary [secondary] ) }
        [MASTERPW(password)]
        [READPW(password)]
        UPDATEPW(password)]
        )
        [CATALOG(mastercatalog[/password] ) ]
```

The following are required parameters:

NAME   The value coded for *entryname* is the name that must be used in all future references to the user catalog. *entryname* may consist of one to 44 characters. These characters may be A-Z, 0-9, @, #,

101

$, - (the hyphen) and the 12/0 overpunch (hex C0). Names containing more than eight characters must be separated by a period; between each period, one to eight characters may be coded. The first character of an *entryname* must be A-Z, @, # or $. The *entryname* is also coded as the file-ID of the DLBL statement.

FILE   Specifies the *filename* coded on the DLBL statement; the latter must be included in the JCL used to execute IDCAMS and the DEFINE USERCATALOG command. The *filename* may consist of one to seven alphanumeric characters, the first of which must be alphabetic.

VOLUME   May be abbreviated as VOL. Specifies the DASD volume that is to contain the user catalog. This volume cannot be owned by any other VSAM catalog.

As before, the following four parameters control allocation of physical space. You may choose whichever option you like best, but one of the four must be selected. Both *primary* and *secondary* allocation can be made. These values may be expressed in decimal, hexadecimal or binary. Values expressed in hexadecimal must be preceded by X; values expressed in binary must be preceded by B. Hexadecimal and binary values must also be enclosed in single quotation marks and cannot be longer than one full word.

BLOCKS   Specifies how many FBA blocks are to be allocated. Supported for FBA devices only.

CYLINDERS   May be abbreviated as CYL. Specifies the number of cylinders to be allocated.

RECORDS   May be abbreviated as REC. Specifies the number of records for which space is to be allocated. Each record contained in a user catalog consists of 512 bytes.

TRACKS   May be abbreviated as TRK. Specifies the number of tracks to be allocated.

The following are four optional parameters that deal with password protection. A *password* may consist of one to eight EBCDIC characters. If it contains commas, semicolons, blanks, parentheses or slashes, the password must be enclosed in single quotation marks. If you include a single quotation mark within a password, it must be coded as two single quotation marks whenever the password is enclosed in single quotation marks.

Passwords can be expressed in hexadecimal. Two hexadecimal characters represent one EBCDIC character. The hexadecimal value must be preceded by X and enclosed in single quotation marks.

MASTERPW   May be abbreviated as MRPW. Specifies a master level password for the user catalog. If any files connected to the catalog are password protected, a master password must be present. The master password allows all I/O operations.

READPW   May be abbreviated as RDPW. Specifies a read level password for the user catalog. The read password permits read operations only.

UPDATEPW   May be abbreviated as UPDPW. Specifies an update level password for the user catalog. The update password permits both read and write operations.

CATALOG   May be abbreviated as CAT. *mastercatalog* specifies the name of the master catalog. The *password* parameter refers to the highest level of password available at the master catalog level. If the master catalog is password protected, this parameter must be included with the DEFINE USERCATALOG command.

Applications programmers are much more likely to define user catalogs rather than a master catalog. The latter is typically controlled by systems programmers. Because of this responsibility difference, I waited until user catalogs were introduced before discussing how to allocate space to a catalog.

TRACKS(75 15)

According to this example, VSAM will initially allocate 75 tracks of physical DASD space. What if the catalog exceeds 75 tracks? That's where the secondary allocation comes into play. In our example, an additional 15 tracks would be allocated.

For CKD devices, it doesn't really matter whether you use the CYLINDERS, RECORDS or TRACKS parameter. Regardless of which one you code, VSAM automatically converts it to tracks.

For FBA devices, the BLOCKS or RECORDS parameter may be coded.

Rarely will you be able to calculate the exact amount of space that a catalog requires, but please make an attempt—don't just pull numbers out of thin air! The steps I recommend taking are:

1) Estimate how many records the catalog will contain. A good rule of thumb is three records for each KSDS or AI plus an additional record if the AI is upgradeable; two records for each ESDS or RRDS; and one for each path, space and volume. Once you derive an estimate, I urge you to up it generously.

2) Determine how many control areas will be needed for the data component of the cluster. All three VSAM structures consist of a data component. However, the KSDS structure also supports an index component. As you can see from the following chart, the DASD model affects CA estimates.

DASD Model	Record Capacity of a CA
3330	40
3340	48
3350	54
3375	80
3380	92

Refer to the IBM manual DOS/VS Access Method Services User's Guide (GC33-5382) for a sample worksheet which can further help you determine catalog size.

Like all AMS functions, IDCAMS must be executed for the DEFINE USERCATALOG command. By the way, I strongly recommend that the DLBL and EXTENT statements for the master catalog be placed in the standard label area. Thus, it won't be necessary to include these JCL statements when you're dealing with other commands (such as the DEFINE USER-CATALOG) that need access to the master catalog.

Now, back to the special JCL coding requirements for the DEFINE USERCATALOG command. The filename coded on the DLBL statement must be identical to the one used in the command's FILE parameter. The volume coded in the NAME parameter must be used as the DLBL's file-ID. Include an ASSGN statement for the logical unit specified in the VOLUME parameter. This same logical unit needs to be referenced on an EXTENT statement. The BLOCKS, CYLINDERS, TRACKS or RECORDS parameter controls the physical allocations specified with the EXTENT statement.

```
/ /   JOB USERCAT
/ /   ASSGN SYS012,CKD,VOL = DATA01,SHR
/ /   DLBL USERCAT,'VSAM.USER.CAT',,VSAM
/ /   EXTENT SYS012,DATA01,1,0,12,1200
/ /   EXEC IDCAMS,SIZE = AUTO
      DEFINE   USERCATALOG                    -
               (NAME(VSAM.USER.CAT)           -
               FILE(USERCAT)                  -
               VOLUME(DATA01)                 -
               TRACKS(1200)
/ *
/ &
```

This example is about as basic as you can get. When you actually establish a user catalog, you'll probably want to include other parameters, such as password protection. VSAM also affords you with the ability to issue AMS commands pertinent only to data or index components.

DEFINE SPACE

The DEFINE SPACE command (DEF SPC) is used to define VSAM data space or to reserve DASD volumes for future VSAM usage. Before a VSAM file can be loaded to DASD, both the space and the cluster must be defined. However, a DEFINE SPACE

105

command isn't actually issued for individual VSAM files. Once VSAM has been assigned space via the DEFINE SPACE command, it then automatically suballocates this space for the different files using it. That's part of the disk management facility that VSAM is so noted for!

The unit of space over which the DEFINE SPACE command gives VSAM control is called a *data space*. If VSAM owns data space, this space can be used only by VSAM. In other words, don't try to restore a DAM file in this area of DASD. A common way many describe this VSAM data space is as a pool from which VSAM allocates space for data sets it manages.

VSAM can own more than one data space on a volume. It can also own data space on several volumes. However, the same VSAM space cannot start on one volume and then continue to another.

DEFINE SPACE
    [FILE (filename)
     VOLUMES(volser [volser . . .])
     {BLOCKS (primary [secondary])|
     CYLINDERS(primary [secondary])|
     RECORDS(primary [secondary])|
     TRACKS(primary [secondary])}
    [RECORDSIZE(average maximum)]
    [CATALOG(catname[/password][filename])]

The following are required parameters:

FILE   Specifies the *filename* coded on the DLBL statement; the latter must be included in the JCL used to execute IDCAMS and the DEFINE SPACE command. The *filename* may consist of one to seven alphanumeric characters, the first of which must be alphabetic.

VOLUMES May be abbreviated as VOL. Multiple volumes may be referenced with this parameter. It specifies the DASD volumes that are to be defined as available VSAM space.

As before, the following four parameters control allocation of physical space. You may choose whichever option you like best, but one of the four must be selected. Both *primary* and *secondary* allocations may be made. These values can be expressed in decimal, hexadecimal or binary. Values expressed in hexadecimal must be preceded by X; values expressed in binary must be preceded by B. Hexadecimal and binary values must also be enclosed in single quotation marks and cannot be longer than one full word.

BLOCKS   Specifies how many FBA blocks are to be allocated. Supported for FBA devices only.

CYLINDERS May be abbreviated as CYL. Specifies the number of cylinders to be allocated.

RECORDS   May be abbreviated as REC. Specifies the number of records for which space is to be allocated. The RECORDSIZE parameter enables AMS to calculate the amount of space needed.

TRACKS   May be abbreviated as TRK. Specifies the number of tracks to be allocated.

The following parameter is required only if allocation is being made in terms of RECORDS.

RECORDSIZE May be abbreviated as RECSZ. Specifies the average and maximum record size of the VSAM records that will occupy this space. Used by VSAM to determine how much space to allocate if the RECORDS parameter is specified. *average* and *maximum* values can be expressed in decimal, hexadecimal or binary. Values expressed in hexadecimal must be preceded by X; values expressed in binary must be preceded by B. Hexadecimal and binary values must also be enclosed in single quotation marks and cannot be longer than one full word.

The following is an optional parameter:

DOS VSAM for Application Programmers

CATALOG May be abbreviated as CAT. *catname* specifies the
name of the catalog that will contain the space. If
the catalog is password protected, the respective
password must be included with this parameter.
filename specifies the same used on the DLBL
statement for the catalog being referenced. If the
catalog is the job catalog, the *filename* may be
omitted since IJSYSUC is assumed; if a job catalog
is not used, VSAM assumes you are referencing the
master catalog. Although this parameter is optional
and a default to the job catalog can be assumed, we
recommend that you include it for the sake of good
internal documentation.

Again, let's assume that the DLBL and EXTENT statements
for the master catalog are in the standard label area. The
filename coded on the DLBL statement must agree with the value given for the FILE parameter. The VOLUMES parameter
controls the logical units that will be assigned.

```
/ /  JOB SPACE
/ /  ASSGN SYS012,CKD,VOL = DATA01,SHR
/ /  DLBL SPACE01,'VSAM.SPACE.DATA01',,VSAM
/ /  EXTENT SYSO12,DATA01,1,0,12,1200
/ /  DLBL USERCAT /VSAM.USER.CAT',,VSAM
/ /  EXTENT SYS012,DATA01
/ /  EXEC IDCAMS,SIZE = AUTO
     DEFINE    SPACE                          -
               (FILE(SPACE01)                 -
               VOLUMES(DATA01)                -
               TRACKS(1200) )
               CATALOG(VSAM,USER,CAT    USERCAT)
/ *
```

DEFINE CLUSTER

The DEFINE CLUSTER command (DEF CL) is used to define
a file to be written to the VSAM catalog. When you execute
IDCAMS for a DEFINE CLUSTER command, the DASD volume
that is to contain the file does not have to be mounted. Howev-

108

er, once you are ready to actually load the file, then it must be available.

Regardless of VSAM organizational structures, the DEFINE CLUSTER command is used. The only difference is how you go about structuring this command. For a KSDS, three entries are created in the catalog:

1) Entry for the cluster.
2) Data component.
3) Index component.

For an ESDS or RRDS, two entries are created in the catalog:

1) Entry for the cluster.
2) Data component.

Let's take a look at the basic format for a cluster definition. Although we've elected to include only the more common ones, numerous parameters are available. If your data center does not have standards regarding catalogs and clusters, I strongly recommend that such standards be developed. In fact, VSAM even has a facility which allows you to model new cluster definitions after existing ones. The MODEL parameter, which we'll explore later in this discussion, assists in this process.

```
DEFINE CLUSTER
        (NAME(entryname)
        VOLUMES(volser [volser . . .])
        {BLOCKS(primary [secondary]) |
        CYLINDERS(primary [secondary]) |
        RECORDS(primary [secondary]) |
        TRACKS(primary [secondary])}
        [ATTEMPTS(number)]
        [BUFFERSPACE(bufsize)]
        [CONTROLINTERVALSIZE(cisize)]
        [FREESPACE [cipercent [(capercent])]]
        [IMBED|NOIMBED]
        [INDEXED|NONINDEXED|NUMBERED]
        [KEYS(length offset)]
```

```
            [KEYRANGES((lowkey highkey)...)]
            [ORDERED|UNORDERED]
            [READPW(password)]
            [RECORDSIZE(average maximum)]
            [RECOVERY|SPEED]
            [REPLICATE|NOREPLICATE]
            [SHAREOPTIONS(crosspartition [crosssystem])]
            [UPDATEPW(password)]
            [WRITECHECK|NOWRITECHECK]
            )
[DATA
            (NAME(entryname)
            {BLOCKS(primary[secondary])|
            CYLINDERS(primary[secondary])|
            RECORDS(primary[secondary])|
            TRACKS(primary[secondary])}
            [RECORDSIZE(average maximum)]
            [SHAREOPTIONS(crosspartition[crosssystem])]
            )]
[INDEX
            (NAME(entryname)
            {BLOCKS(primary[secondary])|
            CYLINDERS(primary [secondary])|
            RECORDS(primary[secondary])|
            TRACKS(primary[secondary])}
            [SHAREOPTIONS(crosspartition[crosssystem])]
            )]
            [CATALOG(catname[/password][filename])]
```

The format example repeats some of the parameters of the data and index component levels of the cluster. Actually, most of the parameters available at the main cluster level are also allowed for defining data and index components. Why place them on a component level? Perhaps the same rules don't apply to each aspect of the cluster you want to define. For example, you might wish to choose separate physical allocations for the data and index areas of a KSDS.

The following are required parameters. With the exception of the NAME parameter, these parameters can be specified at the cluster or data level. Depending on the file's organizational structure, they can also be specified at the index level.

NAME   The value coded for *entryname* is the name that must be used in all future references to the cluster or component it's associated with. *entryname* can consist of one to 44 characters; A-Z, 0-9, @, #, $, - (the hyphen), and the 12/0 overpunch (hex C0). Names containing more than eight characters must be separated by a period; between each period, one to eight characters can be coded. The first character of an entryname must be A-Z, @, #, or $. NAME must be specified at the cluster level. You may optionally specify it for a data or index component. If you do not code this parameter at the component level, a name is automatically generated and listed.

VOLUMES Can be abbreviated VOL. Multiple volumes can be referenced with this parameter, which specifies the DASD volumes that are to contain the cluster or component. VOLUMES must be specified at the cluster or data component level, or at both the data and index component levels.

The following parameters control allocation of physical space. You may choose whichever option you like best, but one of the four must be used.

Both primary and secondary allocations may be made. These values can be expressed in decimal, hexadecimal, or binary form. Values expressed in hexadecimal must be preceded by X; values expressed in binary must be preceded by B. Hexadecimal and binary values must also be enclosed in single quotation marks and cannot be longer than one full word.

BLOCKS   Specifies how many FBA blocks are to be allocated. Supported for FBA devices only.

CYLINDERS Abbreviated CYL; specifies the number of cylinders to be allocated.

RECORDS   Abbreviated REC; specifies the number of records for which space is to be allocated.

TRACKS   Abbreviated TRK; specifies the number of tracks to be allocated.

Size-related parameters can be specified at either the cluster or data component level, or at both the data and index component levels. If you provide for a secondary allocation at the data level, you must also provide for it at the index level if you do not provide at the cluster level.

The following are optional parameters:

ATTEMPTS Abbreviated ATT; specifies the maximum number of times the computer operator can try to enter a correct password. Prompting messages will be issued by AMS. *number* can have a value of 0 through 7. If this parameter is not coded, a default value of 2 is assumed.

BUFFERSPACE(bufsize) Abbreviated BUFSPC or BUFSP; specifies the minimum space to be allocated for buffers. *bufsize* is expressed in terms of numbers of bytes, and cannot be less than enough space to contain two data component CIs and, if it's a KSDS, one index component CI.

CONTROLINTERVALSIZE(cisize) Abbreviated CNVSZ or CISZ; specifies in bytes the size of the control intervals. CI size for a data component can range from 512 to 32,768 bytes. If the size is between 512 and 8192, CI size must be a multiple of 512. If the size is between 8192 and 32,768, CI size must be a multiple of 2048. CI size for an index component can be 512, 1024, 2048, or 4096. If you code an incorrect value, VSAM automatically chooses the next highest multiple.

FREESPACE Abbreviated FSPC, it is supported for a KSDS only. FSPC specifies as percentages the amount of free space for each CI and CA in the file. If this parameter is not coded, a default value of 0 is assumed.

IMBED|NOIMBED Abbreviated IMBD and NIMBD, respectively, and supported for a KSDS only. IMBED specifies that the lowest level of the index (also referred to as the *sequence set*) is to be stored in the file's data component. If it's to be stored in the index component, NOIMBED must be specified. The default value is NOIMBED. This parameter can be responsible for some real performance improvements. Although IMBED uses more DASD space, it will provide better machine utilization if you do not have enough real storage to keep most or all of the index in storage during program execution.

INDEXED|NONINDEXED|NUMBERED   Abbreviated IXD, NIXD, and NUMD, respectively. Specifies the file's organizational structure.

> KSDS: INDEXED
> ESDS: NONINDEXED
> RRDS: NUMBERED

The default value is INDEXED. If INDEXED is specified or assumed, an index component is automatically defined and placed in the catalog.

KEYRANGES   Abbreviated KRNG; applies to a KSDS only. This parameter provides you with a way to place portions of a KSDS on different DASD volumes. To actually use this parameter, multiple volumes must be used for the cluster. *lowkey* specifies the low key of the range; *highkey* specifies the high key of the range.

KEYS   Supported for a KSDS only. Specifies attributes of the key field. *length* is expressed in bytes and can be a value of 1 through 255. *offset* is the key's starting position in the logical record, relative to 0. For example, if the key is the first field contained in a record, then the offset entry is 0. These values need to agree with the way the key is logically described in the application programs.

ORDERED|UNORDERED   Abbreviated ORD and UNORD, respectively. ORDERED indicates that the allocated DASD volumes are to be used in the order in which they are listed on the VOLUMES parameter. The default value is UNORDERED.

READPW   Abbreviated RDPW; specifies a read level password for the cluster or component. The read level password permits read operations only.

RECORDSIZE   Abbreviated RECSZ; specifies the average and maximum record size of data records. Assists VSAM in the calculation of CI and CA areas. For an RRDS, average and maximum values must be equal. The default for both values is 4089. Because this number is probably highly inaccurate when compared with the true physical size of your file, you should code this parameter for better machine utilization.

RECOVERY|SPEED   The former may be abbreviated as RCVY. Determines whether the allocated DASD area is to be preformatted before records are loaded. (This applies only when the file is initially loaded.) SPEED indicates that the space is not to be preformatted. RECOVERY indicates that the space is to be preformatted. The default value is RECOVERY. If SPEED is coded, your file will be loaded considerably faster. However, if the load fails, it must be restarted from the beginning. On the other hand, RECOVERY allows a quick restart if a load fails, since the restore will be restarted at the point of failure.

REPLICATE|NOREPLICATE   Abbreviated as REPL and NREPL, respectively. Applies to a KSDS only. REPLICATE directs each index record to be written on a track as many times as it will fit, which helps reduce rotational delay and improve performance. The default value is NOREPLICATE.

SHAREOPTIONS   Abbreviated SHR; specifies how a cluster can be shared across partitions or systems. Valid values are 1, 2, 3, and 4. For an in-depth explanation of these codes, refer to Figs. 7-1 and 7-2. The default for *cross-partition* is 1; the default for *cross-system* is 3.

UPDATEPW   Abbreviated UPDPW, specifies an update level password for the catalog or component. The update password permits both read and write operations.

WRITECHECK|NOWRITECHECK   Abbreviated WCK and NWCK, respectively. This parameter determines whether VSAM is to check the data transfer of records.

CROSS-PARTITION SHARE OPTION

Partitions can share access to VSAM files. This is controlled by cross-partition share options. Valid codes are 1, 2, 3 and 4. To describe these codes, we use the term "input" to refer to read operations only. "Output" refers to write operations.

Share option 4 is not supported for an ESDS. If specified, it is ignored and a default value of 1 is assumed.

Code 1 Jobs running in any number of partitions can access the file simultaneously with the restriction that all jobs must open the file for input only. If one job opens the file for output, no other job can open the same file. This option ensures you full read/write integrity.

Code 2 Jobs running in any number of partitions can access the file simultaneously with the restriction that only one job can open the file for output. Any other job accessing the file must use it for input only. This option ensures write integrity only since the file can be modified by jobs in other partitions while records are being retrieved from it.

Code 3 Jobs running in any number of partitions can access the file simultaneously for both input and output activity. This option ensures neither read nor write integrity. Several jobs can add records to the file at the same time.

Code 4 Jobs running in any number of partitions can access the file simultaneously for both input and output activity. However, the following restrictions apply:

A CA split is not allowed.

Data cannot be added to an end-of-file.

This option provides both read and write integrity. However, this consumes significant processor resources and may also result in additional I/Os.

FIG. 7-1. Cross-Partition Share Options

WRITECHECK tests for a data check condition by writing a record and then reading it. If NO-WRITECHECK is specified, the record is written but not followed by a read test. The default value is NOWRITECHECK.

CROSS-SYSTEM SHARE OPTIONS

DOS does not support cross-system sharing. However, if a VSAM file is created in a DOS environment and then imported into an MVS system, then this parameter is effective. If you have no plans for transporting the file into a different operating system, it does not matter which option is selected.

Code 3 Jobs running in any number of systems can access the file simultaneously for both input and output activity. However, this option ensures neither read nor write integrity.

Code 4 Jobs running in any number of systems can access the file simultaneously for both input and output activity. However, the following restrictions apply:

A CA split is not allowed.
Data cannot be added to an end-of-file.
This option provides both read and write integrity. However, this consumes significant processor resources and many also result in additional I/Os.

FIG. 7-2. Cross-System Share Options

CATALOG   Abbreviated CAT and specified at the cluster level only. *catname* specifies the name of the catalog in which the cluster is to be defined. If the catalog is password protected, the respective password must be included with this parameter. filename specifies the same used on the DLBL statement for the catalog being referenced.

To save coding effort, store DLBL and EXTENT statements for both the master and user catalog in the standard label area. The following is an example of a KSDS cluster definition:

```
//   JOB KSDSDEF
*    CATALOG JCL IS HOUSED IN STANDARD LABEL AREA
//   EXEC IDCAMS,SIZE = AUTO
     DEFINE CLUSTER                        -
               (NAME(INV.MASTER.FILE)      -
               VOL(335005 335011 335012)   -
               INDEXED                     -
               KEYS(9 1 )                  -
```

```
        SPEED                                -
        RECORDS(1350 1350)                   -
        FREESPACE(25 25)                     -
        REUSE  )                             -
DATA -
        (NAME(INV.MASTER.FILE.DATA)          -
        SHAREOPTIONS(4 3)                    -
        RECORDSIZE(300 300))                 -
INDEX -
        (NAME(INV.MASTER.FILE.INDEX)         -
        SHAREOPTIONS(4 3))                   -
     CATALOG(VSAM.USER.CAT   USERCAT)
/*
/&
```

Following is an example of a ESDS cluster definition:

```
//   JOB ESDSDEF
*    CATALOG JCL IS HOUSED IN STANDARD LABEL AREA
//   EXEC IDCAMS, SIZE = AUTO
DEFINE CLUSTER -
        (NAME(INV.TRAN.FILE)-
        VOL (335005 335011 335012)          -
        NONINDEXED                          -
        SPEED                               -
        RECORDS                             -
        RECORDS(250 250)                    -
        FREESPACE(25 25)                    -
        SHAREOPTIONS(4 3)                   -
        REUSE  )                            -
DATA
        (NAME(INV.TRAN.FILE.DATA)           -
        SHAREOPTIONS(4 3)                   -
        RECORDSIZE(80 80)                   -
     CATALOG(VSAM.USER.CAT   USERCAT)
/*
/&
```

The following is an example of an RRDS cluster definition:

```
//    JOB RRDSDEF
*     CATALOG JCL IS HOUSED IN STANDARD LABEL AREA
//    EXEC IDCAMS,SIZE = AUTO
      DEFINE CLUSTER -
            (NAME(INV.ACCT.EXT)              -
            VOL(335005 335011 335012)        -
            NUMBERED                         -
            SPEED                            -
            RECORDS(1OOO)                    -
            RECORDSIZE(150 150)              -
            SHAREOPTIONS(2))                 -
            CATALOG(VSAM.USER.CAT   USERCAT)
/*
/&
```

AMS supports a MODEL parameter for the DEFINE CLUS-
TER command. MODEL allows you to copy attributes from an
existing cluster by coding the name of an existing cluster in the
MODEL parameter:

The cluster to be referenced is ESDS.MODEL.CLUSTER. If
you include this cluster with a DEFINE CLUSTER command,
any parameters present but not included in the command code
will be retrieved from the model.

Some data centers create *default models*. These clusters
never have any space allocated to them; their only purpose is
to serve as models for other clusters. These types of clusters also
have reserved names.

DEFAULT.MODEL.KSDS
DEFAULT.MODEL.ESDS
DEFAULT.MODEL.RRDS

Talk with your systems programming staff about default
models. They can save everyone coding effort and, even more
importantly, ensure the inclusion of better performance parameters and more standardization.

DEFINE ALTERNATEINDEX

The DEFINE ALTERNATEINDEX command (DEF AIX) is used to define alternate indexes. Both the KSDS and ESDS organizational structures support AIs. An AI is related to an existing base cluster through the DEFINE ALTERNATEINDEX command. The BLDINDEX command, which we'll discuss shortly, creates the AI.

```
DEFINE ALTERNATEINDEX
      (NAME(entryname)
      RELATE(entryname/password)
      VOLUMES(volser[ volser...])
      {BLOCKS(primary[ secondary])|
      CYLINDERS(primary[secondary])|
      RECORDS(primary[secondary])|
      TRACKS(primary[secondary])}
      [KEYS(length offset)]
      [UNIQUEKEY | NONUNIQUEKEY]
          )
      CATALOG(catname[/password][filename]))]
```

The following are required parameters:

NAME   The value coded for entryname is the name that must be used in all future references to the AI. entryname can consist of one to 44 characters: A-Z, 0-9, @, #, $, - (the hyphen), and the 12/0 overpunch (hex C0). Names containing more than eight characters must be separated by a period; between each period, one to eight characters can be coded. The first character of an entryname must be A-Z, @, #, or $.

RELATE   Abbreviated REL. The value coded for entryname is the name of the cluster to which the AI is related. In other words, this parameter establishes the relationship between an AI and a cluster. If the cluster is password-protected, you must code password with the appropriate value.

VOLUMES Abbreviated VOL. Multiple volumes can be referenced with this parameter, which specifies the DASD volumes that are to contain the AI.

119

The following parameters control allocation of physical space. You can choose whichever option you like best, but you must select one of the four.

Both primary and secondary allocations may be made. These values can be expressed in decimal, hexadecimal, or binary form. Values expressed in hexadecimal must be preceded by X; values expressed in binary must be preceded by B. Hexadecimal and binary values must also be enclosed in single quotation marks and cannot be longer than one full word.

BLOCKS   Specifies how many FBA blocks are to be allocated. Supported for FBA devices only.

CYLINDERS   Abbreviated CYL: specifies the number of cylinders to be allocated.

RECORDS   Abbreviated REC: specifies the number of records for which space is to be allocated.

TRACKS   Abbreviated as TRK: specifies the number of tracks to be allocated.

Following are optional parameters:

KEYS   Specifies attributes of the AI field within the cluster. length is expressed in bytes and can be any value from 1 through 255. offset is the alternate key's starting position in the logical record relative to 0. For example, if the alternate key is the first field contained in a record, the offset entry is 0. These values need to agree with the way the alternate key is logically described in the application programs.

UNIQUEKEY|NONUNIQUEKEY   Abbreviated as UNQK and NUNQK, respectively. UNIQUEKEY specifies that duplicate keys are not allowed; each record's AI must have a unique value. NONUNIQUEKEY supports duplicate AIs; multiple records may have the same value for an AI. The default value is NONUNIQUEKEY.

CATALOG   Abbreviated as CAT. catname specifies the name of the catalog housing the cluster named in the RELATE parameter. If the catalog is password-protected, the respective *password* must be included with this parameter. *filename* specifies the same used on the DLBL statement for the catalog being referenced.

Reduce your JCL coding effort for IDCAMS by storing the DLBL and EXTENT statements for both the master and user catalogs in the standard label area.

The following is an example of an AI definition:

```
//   JOB AIDEF
*    CATALOG JCL IS HOUSED IN STANDARD LABEL AREA
/ /  EXEC IDCAMS,SIZE = AUTO
     DEFINE ALTERNATEINDEX              -
          (NAME(INV.MASTER.AIX)         -
          RELATE(INV.MASTER.FILE)       -
          VOL(335005 335011 335012)     -
          TRACKS(48 24)                 -
          KEYS(3 10)                    -
          UNIQUEKEY )                   -
     CATALOG(VSAM.USER.CAT   USERCAT)
/*
/&
```

DEFINE PATH

The DEFINE PATH command (DEF PATH) is used to define a *path*, which is the mechanism VSAM used to travel through an AI to the related base cluster. Before you define a path, you must define the AI.

```
DEFINE PATH
     (NAME(entryname)
     PATHENTRY(entryname[/password])
     )
[CATALOG(catname[/password][filename])]
```

The following are required parameters:

NAME   The value coded for *entryname* is the name that must be used in all future references to the path.

entryname can consist of one to 44 characters. These characters may be A-Z, 0-9, @, #, $, - (the hyphen), and the 12/0 overpunch (hex C0.) Names containing more than eight characters must be separated by a period; between each period, one to eight characters may be coded. The first character of an *entryname* must be A-Z, @, #, or $.

PATHENTRY Abbreviated PENT. The value coded for *entryname* is the name of the AI to which the path is related. If the AI is password protected, you must code *password* with the appropriate value.

The following is an optional parameter:

CATALOG Abbreviated CAT. *catname* specifies as the name of the catalog housing the AI named in the PATHENTRY parameter. If the catalog is password protected, the respective *password* must be included with this parameter. *filename* specifies the same used on the DLBL statement for the catalog being referenced.

Storing DLBL and EXTENT statements for both the master and user catalogs in the standard label area will save JCL coding effort. Following is an example of a path definition:

```
// JOB PATHDEF
*  CATALOG JCL IS HOUSED IN STANDARD LABEL AREA
// EXEC IDCAMS,SIZE = AUTO
   DEFINE PATH
          (NAME(INV.MASTER.PATH)              -
          PATHENTRY(INV.MASTER.AIX))          -
   CATALOG(VSAM.USER.CAT   USERCAT)
/*
/&
```

DELETE

The DELETE command (DEL) is used to delete clusters, space, catalogs, alternate indexes, and paths. When some objects are deleted, others are automatically removed. The following summarizes what type of action actually takes place when a DELETE is issued.

DELETE CLUSTER   Deletes data component, index component, alternate indexes, and paths.

DELETE ALTERNATEINDEX   Deletes alternate index and paths. Related base cluster is unaffected.

DELETE PATH   Deletes path. Related alternate index and base cluster are unaffected.

DELETE USERCATALOG   Deletes user catalog but it must be empty.

Now let's take a look at the format used for the DELETE command.

```
DELETE (entryname[/password][entryname[/password]...]
       [entrytype]
       [CATALOG(catname[/password][filename])]
       [FORCE|NOFORCE]
       [PURGE|NOPURGE]
       [ERASE|NOERASE]
```

The following is a required parameter:

entryname   The value coded for entryname is the name of the object to be deleted. If applicable, the object's password also must be included. More than one object may be deleted in a command statement.

The following are optional parameters:

entrytype   Specifies the type of entries to be deleted. If the entrytype parameter is coded, the object named in the entryname parameter must belong to the specified type, or the DELETE command is terminated. Furthermore, when the entrytype parameter is used, only objects belonging to one type can be deleted in each command statement. Valid values are:

ALTERNATEINDEX or AIX
CLUSTER or CL
MASTERCATALOG or MCAT
PATH - - - - - - - -
SPACE or SPC
USERCATALOG or UCAT

CATALOG   Abbreviated CAT. catname specifies the name of the catalog housing the objects to be deleted. When a master or user catalog is deleted, however, this parameter cannot be used. If the catalog is password protected, the respective password must be included with this parameter. filename specifies the same used on the DLBL statement for the catalog being referenced. If the CATALOG parameter is omitted, the master catalog is assumed.

FORCE|NOFORCE   Abbreviated as FRC and NFRC, respectively. Applicable only if SPACE is coded as the entrytype. FORCE results in a deletion of data space even if it contains clusters. NOFORCE results in a deletion of empty data space only. The default value is NOFORCE.

PURGE|NOPURGE   Abbreviated as PRG and NPRG, respectively. PURGE deletes an object even if its retention period has not expired. NOPURGE deletes an object only if the retention period has expired. The default value is NOPURGE.

ERASE|NOERASE   Abbreviated ERAS and NERAS, respectively. Applicable only when an alternate index or cluster is deleted. ERASE writes over the data component with binary zeros. NOERASE does not overlay the data component with binary zeros. The default value is the option specified in the most recent DEFINE or ALTER command for the object.

124

JCL coding requirements can be reduced if you store DLBL and EXTENT statements for both the master and user catalogs in the standard label area.

```
/ / JOB CLDEL    CLUSTER DELETE
* CATALOG JCL IS HOUSED IN STANDARD LABEL AREA
/ / EXEC IDCAMS,SIZE = AUTO
DELETE (INV.MASTER.FILE) -
CLUSTER PURGE -
CATALOG(VSAM.USER.CAT USERCAT)
/*
/&
```

ALTER

The ALTER command is used to change an object's attributes. One good example of an attribute is the DASD volumes used to store the object. The ALTER command can be used to add or delete volumes.

What if you execute an ALTER command but omit some of the parameters specified when the object was originally defined? Any attribute omitted from an ALTER command remains unchanged. For example, if you don't alter the password then it stays the same.

```
ALTER entryname[/password]
    [CATALOG(name[/password])]
    [NEWNAME(entryname)]
    [ADDVOLUMES(volser...)]
    [REMOVEVOLUMES(volser...)]
```

The following is a required parameter:

entryname   The value coded for entryname is the name of the object to be altered. If applicable, the object's password also must be included.

The following are optional parameters:

CATALOG   Abbreviated CAT. catname specifies the name of the catalog housing the object to be altered. If the catalog is password protected, the respective password must be included with this parameter. filename specifies the same used on the DLBL statement for the catalog being referenced.

NEWNAME specifies a new name for the object. The value coded for this parameter becomes the entryname for all future references (i.e., DELETE). entryname may consist of one to 44 characters. These characters may be A-Z, 0-9, @, #, $, - (the hyphen), and 12/0 overpunch (hex C0). Names containing more than eight characters must be separated by a period; between each period, one to eight characters may be coded. The first character of an entryname must be A-Z, @, #, or $.

ADDVOLUMES Adds DASD Volumes to the available space pool. More than one *volser* may be specified.

REMOVE VOLUMES Removes DASD volumes from the available space pool. More than one *volser* may be specified.

This time we barely scratched the surface of available parameters. Nearly all parameters available with the DEFINE CLUSTER command are also available when executing an ALTER. That's the idea behind the ALTER: it provides you with an easy way to change cluster-related parameters.

Again, I recommend streamlining the JCL coding effort by storing DLBL and EXTENT statements for both the master and user catalogs in the standard label area.

```
//    JOB ALTER
*     CATALOG JCL IS HOUSED IN STANDARD LABEL AREA
//    EXEC IDCAMS,SIZE = AUTO
      ALTER INV.TRANS.FILE              -
      NEWNAME(INV.TRANS)                -
      ADDVOLUMES(335020 335021)
/*
/&
```

BLDINDEX

The BLDINDEX command (BIX) is used to build one or more alternate indexes over a base cluster. Before this command can be successfully executed, both the alternate index and the base cluster must be defined and related to each other by a path. The cluster must be loaded.

```
BLDINDEX INFILE(filename[/password])
         OUTFILE(filename[/password])
```

The following are required parameters:

INFILE   Abbreviated IFILE. filename specifies the same used on the DLBL statement for either the related path or the base cluster. If the path's filename is specified, the path's password must also be coded if present. In the case of a base cluster, any password level may be used.

OUTFILE   Abbreviated as OFILE. filename specifies the same used on the DLBL statement for either the alternate index or path to be built. If the AI is password protected, the update or higher-level password must also be coded if present. In the case of a path, the path's password may be used.

Note that the JCL coding example differs substantially from previous ones. This time we included DLBL and EXTENT statements for a base cluster, as well as an alternate index. For catalog assignments, we chose to again rely on the standard label area.

```
// JOB BLDIND
// ASSGN SYS007,DISK,VOL = VSER01,SHR
// DLBL INVDD,'INV.MASTER.FILE',,VSAM
// EXTENT SYS007,VSER01
// DLBL AIDD,'INV.MASTER.AI',,VSAM
// EXTENT SYS007,VSER01
// EXEC IDCAMS,SIZE = AUTO
   BLDINDEX -
   INFILE(INVDD) -
   OUTFILE(AIDD/AIUPPW)
/*
/&
```

```
LISTING OF DATA SET -INV.TRAN.FILE

RBA OF RECORD - 0
0000  00030000 00000000 000030F1 F0F1F2F8   F6000000 00000000
0020  00030000 00000000 00033000 00030000   00000000 00000000
0040  0C000000 00000000 00000000 00000000

RBA OF RECORD - 80
0000  D4F1F3F0 F0F1F6F0 F1F3F1F1 F0F1F0FB   F6C5D5E5 C5D3D6D7
0020  E84004C1 C9D340C8 E4D9D9C9 C3C1D5C5   40404040 40404040
0040  40404040 F0F0F0F0 F2F5F0F0 F0F0F0F5

RBA OF RECORD - 160
0000  D4F1F3F0 F0F1F6F0 F1F2F1F1 F0F1F0FB   F6F0F0F0 F0F0F2F0
0020  F0F0F0F0 F1F3F5F6 F6F5F0F0 F0F0F0F2   F7F1F3F3 C4D6E4C2
0040  40404040 40404040 40404040 40404040

RBA OF RECORD - 240
0000  D7F1F3F0 F0F6F3F0 F1F3F1F0 F9F0F3F8   F6C9D5E5 D6C9C3C5
0020  C1D5C3C9 C1D340D7 D3C1C3C5 40404040   40404040 40404040
0040  40404040 F0F0F0F0 F0F8F0F0 F0F0F0F2

RBA OF RECORD - 320
0000  D7F1F3F0 F0F6F3F0 F1F2F1F0 F9F0F3F8   F6F0F0F0 F0F0F0F4
0020  F0F0F0F0 F1F5F0F0 F0F0F0F0 F0F0F0F0   F6F0F0F0 D2E5C240
0040  40404040 40404040 40404040 40404040

IDC0005I NUMBER OF RECORDS PROCESSED WAS 5

IDC0001I FUNCTION COMPLETED, HIGHEST CONDITION CODE WAS 0
```

PRINT

The PRINT command is used to display on SYSLST the contents of a VSAM file. All or part of a file may be printed.

```
PRINT INFILE(filename[/password])
    [CHARACTER|DUMP|HEX]
    [FROMADDRESS(address) |
    FROMKEY(key)|
    FROMNUMBER(number)|
    SKIP(count)]
    [TOADDRESS(address)|
```

Sample Output From Print Command

```
00000000 00000000    *...........101286..............*
00000000 00000000    *.............................. *
                     *............... ...            *


C540C2C1 D5D240C2    *M1300160131101086ENVELOPE  BANK  B*
40404040 40404040    *Y  MAIL  HURRICANE                *
                     *     000025000005                 *


C2D6E740 FOFOFOFO    *M1300160121101086 0000020BOX  0000*
D3C54040 40404040    *00001356650000027133DOUBLE        *
                     *                                  *


40D6D5C5 40C6C9D5    *P1300630131090386INVOICE  ONE  FIN*
40404040 40404040    *ANCIAL  PLACE                     *
                     *     000008000002                 *


D7D2C740 FOFOFOFO    *P13006301210903860000004PKG  0000*
D7D9C9D5 E3404040    *00001500000000006000KVB  PRINT   *
                     *                                  *
```

TOKEY(key)|
TONUMBER(number)|
COUNT(count)]

The following is a required parameter:

INFILE   Abbreviated IFILE. filename specifies the same used
on the DLBL statement for the file to be printed. If the
file is password protected, the password parameter must
also be coded. For a catalog, use the read-level password.
For a data component or index component, use the read

or higher-level password of the component, or the master password of the cluster or AI to which the component belongs. For a path, use the path's password.

The following are optional parameters:

CHARACTER|HEX|DUMP   Specifies the format of the output. CHARACTER prints the data in character format. HEX prints the data in hexadecimal format. DUMP prints the data in both character and hexadecimal format. The default value is DUMP.

The following optional parameters determine where the print operation begins. You should only choose one of these options. If you don't specify a starting point, the output from the PRINT command begins with the first record.

FROMADDRESS(address)May be used with KSDS or ESDS files. Specifies the RBA of the logical record where printing is to begin.
FROMKEY(key)   May be used with KSDS files only. Specifies the key of the logical record where printing is to begin. If VSAM cannot locate the specified key, printing begins with the logical record having the next highest key. If the key contains commas, semicolons, blanks, parentheses, or slashes, enclose it in single quotation marks. Code a single quotation mark within a key as two single quotation marks if the key is enclosed in single quotation marks. A key also may be specified in hexadecimal; precede it with an X and enclose the key in single quotation marks.
FROMNUMBER(number)   May be used with RRDS files only. Specifies the relative-record number of the logical record where printing is to begin.
SKIP(count)   May be used with all VSAM files. Specifies the number of records to be skipped before printing begins.

The following optional parameters determine where the print operation ends. Select only one of these options per print

Parameter	File Type	Cannot Be Used in Combination with
FROMADDRESS	KSDS ESDS	TOKEY TONUMBER
FROMKEY	KSDS	TOADDRESS TONUMBER
FROMNUMBER	RRDS	TOADDRESS TOKEY
SKIP	KSDS ESDS RRDS	- - - - - - - - - - - - - - - - - -

FIG. 7-3. Sample Output from Print Command.

operation. If you forget to code an ending point, the output from the PRINT command ends with the last record on file. Also, be aware that if an option is selected for the starting point, it can influence what options are available when coding the ending point. Refer to Fig. 7-3. for details.

TOADDRESS(address)   May be used with KSDS or ESDS files. Specifies the RBA where printing is to end. The RBA does not have to agree with the beginning of a logical record. The entire record containing the specified address is printed as the last output from the command.

TOKEY(key)   May be used with KSDS files only. Specifies the key of the logical record where printing is to end. If VSAM cannot locate the specified key, printing ends with the logical record housing the next lower key. If the key contains commas, semicolons, blanks, parentheses, or slashes, enclose it in single quotation marks. Code a single quotation mark within a key as two single quotation marks if the key is enclosed in single quotation marks. A key also may be specified in hexadecimal; precede it with an X and enclose the key in single quotation marks.

TONUMBER(number) May be used with RRDA files only. Specifies the relative-record number of the logical record where printing is to end.

COUNT(count) May be used with all VSAM files. Specifies the number of records to be listed before the print operation ends.

Following the JCL example is some sample output produced by the PRINT command. I elected to use the DUMP format so that you could see both character and hexadecimal format.

```
/ / JOB PRINT
/ / ASSGN SYS007,DISK,VOL = USER01,SHR
/ / DLBL INVTRAN,'INV.TRAN.FILE', ,VSAM,
/ / EXTENT SYS007,USER01
/ / EXEC IDCAMS,SIZE = AUTO
PRINT INFILE(INVTRAN)             -
        DUMP                      -
        COUNT(5)                  -
/*
/&
```

REPRO

The REPRO command is used to perform the following operations:

- Copy a VSAM file to another VSAM file.
- Copy a SAM file to another file.
- Convert a SAM file to either an ISAM or a VSAM file.
- Convert a VSAM file to either an ISAM or a SAM file.
- Merge two VSAM files.

```
REPRO INFILE(filename)[/password]
    OUTFILE(filename[/password]
    [FROMADDRESS(address)|
    FROMKEY(key)|
    FROMNUMBER(number)|
    SKIP(count)]
    [TOADDRESS(address)|
```

TOKEY(key)|
TONUMBER(number)|
COUNT(count)]

The following are required parameters:

INFILE   Abbreviate IFILE. *filename* specifies the same used on the DLBL or TLBL statement for the input file. If the file is password protected, include the *password*.
OUTFILE   Abbreviated OFILE. *filename* specifies the same used on the DLBL or TLBL statement for the output file. If the file is password protected, include the *password*.

The following optional parameters determine where the copy operation begins. Choose only one of these options. If you don't specify a starting point, the REPRO command begins with the first record on file.

FROMADDRESS(address)   May be used with KSDS or ESDS files. Specifies the RBA of the logical record where copying is to begin.
FROMKEY(key)   May be used with KSDS files and ISAM files. Specifies the key of the logical record where copying is to begin. If VSAM cannot locate the specified key, copying begins with the logical record having the next highest key. If the key contains commas, semicolons, blanks, parentheses, or slashes, enclose it in single quotation marks. Code a single quotation mark within a key as two single quotation marks if the key is enclosed in single quotation marks. A key may also be specified in hexadecimal; precede it with an X and enclose the key in single quotation marks.
FROMNUMBER(number)   May be used with RRDS files only. Specifies the relative-record number of the logical record where copying is to begin.
SKIP(count)   May be used with SAM, ISAM, and VSAM files. Specifies the number of records to be skipped before copying begins.

Parameter	File Type	Cannot Be Used in Combination with
FROMADDRESS	KSDS ESDS	TOKEY TONUMBER
FROMKEY	KSDS ISAM	TOADDRESS TONUMBER
FROMNUMBER	RRDS	TOADDRESS TOKEY
SKIP	KSDS ESDS RRDS ISAM SAM	- -

Fig. 7-4. Repro Restrictions.

The following optional parameters determine where the copy operation ends. Choose only one of these options per copy operation. If you omit coding an ending point, the REPRO command ends with the last record on file. Also, be aware that if an option is selected for the starting point, it can influence what is available when coding this parameter. Refer to Fig. 7-4 for details.

TOADDRESS(address)   May be used with KSDS or ESDS files. Specifies the RBA where copying is to end. The RBA does not have to agree with the beginning of a logical record. The entire record containing the specified address is copied as the last record.

TOKEY(key)   May be used with KSDS files or ISAM files. Specifies the key of the logical record where copying is to end. If the specified key cannot be located, copying ends with the logical record having the next lower key. If the key contains commas, semicolons, blanks, parentheses, or slashes, enclose it in single quotation marks. Code a single quotation mark within a key as two single quotation marks if the key is enclosed in single quotation marks. A key also can be specified in hexadecimal form; precede it with an X and enclose the key in single quotation marks.

TONUMBER(number)   May be used with RRDS files only. Specifies the relative-record number of the logical record where copying is to end.

COUNT(count)   May be used with SAM, ISAM, and VSAM files. Specifies the number of records to be copied before the REPRO operations ends.

These parameters are the basics when it comes to coding a REPRO command. For example, a non-VSAM file may need additional information such as record format and record size. For details about such parameters, refer to IBM's *DOS/VS Access Method Services User's Guide* (GC33-5382).

Now let's take a look at a JCL example for copying one VSAM file to another.

```
// JOB REPRO
// DLBL INVMST,'INV.MASTER.FILE', ,VSAM
// DLBL INVMSTA,'INV.MASTER.FILEA', ,VSAM
// EXEC IDCAMS,SIZE = AUTO
  REPRO INFILE(INVMST)   -
          OUTFILE(INVMSTA)
/*
/&
```

8
CHAPTER

The ISAM
Interface Program

The ISAM Interface Program (popularly referred to as the IIP) is an easy way to make the transition from ISAM to VSAM.

Perhaps your data center has several hundred programs which reference ISAM files. To convert them to native VSAM will require several man-years. At the same time, there is a pressing need to bring in faster DASD models, such as 3380s. The latter cannot support ISAM files. The solution? Use the IIP.

The IIP allows you to convert ISAM files to VSAM but to continue running existing programs without making any changes. The software uses language features applicable to ISAM files, but physically the file is a KSDS VSAM structure. The IIP intercepts all I/O commands. That's how the ISAM/VSAM file-handling differences are managed.

Before I tell you more about the IIP, a few words of advice. The IIP was designed as a conversion aid for users during their migration from ISAM to VSAM. You should view IIPs as temporary measures. IIPs tend to be less efficient than native VSAM processing. Therefore, I do not recommend that you use them any longer than necessary. Furthermore, until your ISAM programs are converted, you will not be able to take advantage of checking the FILE STATUS codes. The FILE STATUS feature offers error-handling capability which is significantly better than ISAM's INVALID KEY logic.

How do you invoke the IIP?

Actually, it's very simple. First, convert the ISAM file to a VSAM file. Since ISAM is based on the idea of indexing by keys, the KSDS structure must be used. The AMS REPRO command may be used to convert the file.

Next, change all JCL statements referencing the ISAM file to VSAM format. Code the DASD statements just the same as if the programs were written in native VSAM. You'll need the same supporting job steps that any other VSAM file needs. By "supporting job steps," I'm referring to such AMS commands as defining user catalogs, data space and clusters. When a program tries to open an ISAM file and finds that its related JCL statement says it's VSAM, the IIP is automatically invoked.

To recap:

1) Convert the file to VSAM using the AMS REPRO command or some other such facility.

2) Use IDCAMS to issue the appropriate AMS commands (i.e., DEF CLUSTER).

3) Replace ASSGN, DLBL and EXTENT statements with DLBL statements in the VSAM format. JCL statements may also be needed for the catalog housing the file entry.

4) Include the SIZE parameter on the EXEC statement.

Let's take an in-depth look at that last step. If you'll recall from your study of DOS JCL, the SIZE parameter must always be specified when executing

1) VSAM programs
2) ISAM programs using the IIP
3) IDCAMS

If you omit this parameter when dealing with any of the above, AMS will terminate your job. For a review of the SIZE parameter, refer to Chapter 5.

RESTRICTIONS

Can any programs which currently reference ISAM files be used with the IIP?

Almost all programs written for ISAM files will successfully run using the IIP. There are some ISAM functions for which no VSAM equivalents exist. There are also ISAM functions which cannot be simulated by the IIP.

Restrictions applicable to IIP usage are:

1) Program must run successfully in an ISAM environment. If it does not work under ISAM, the IIP will not correct the situation.

2) Program must use standard ISAM interfaces.

3) RECORD ID processing is not allowed. VSAM does not support a comparable function.

4) VSAM does not return information applicable to the ERREXT parameter list. Under ISAM, this can be device-dependent information, or the virtual storage or DASD address of the record containing the error.

5) When loading a file, VSAM always assumes that the file is opened in the EXTEND mode. If you try to reload an existing file, VSAM returns a sequence error code. The AMS commands DELETE and DEFINE must be issued before the reload can occur. If it is a reusable file, specify DISP = NEW before attempting a reload.

6) The IIP cannot access a file while it is being used by another program unless VSAM SHAREOPTIONS (3) has been specified. SHAREOPTIONS (4) may also be valid if the records being accessed concurrently are not in the same CA.

7) Files defined with SHAREOPTIONS (4) cannot be shared between IIP users in different systems.

RECORD DELETIONS

A few words about record deletions and the IIP. One of the inefficiencies attributed to ISAM processing is the handling of deletes. Under ISAM, deleted records are not physically removed from the file until it is reorganized.

Unfortunately, ISAM programs running under the IIP share the same weakness. Inactive records remain on the file rather than being physically deleted. Since VSAM files are not reorganized (thus resulting in an automatic removal of such records), other provisions must be made. Otherwise, your VSAM file will continue to retain inactive records, and thus, space is wasted. To solve this problem, write a program to remove those records coded as inactive.

9
CHAPTER

Tuning
Is Important!

Like a piano, VSAM files need to be tuned to make "beautiful music."

Files need to be tuned to perform at their best. If you do not periodically monitor and adjust cluster definitions, they will become less efficient. Both time and DASD resources will be wasted.

In this chapter, I will provide suggestions for improving VSAM performance. A sample monitoring checklist has also been included. I recommend that you take this information and use it as a guideline to develop a policy for your data center. Naturally, there may be changes you want to make, and after you implement a monitoring and tuning effort, more changes may surface.

Change is part of our business. Data processing is definitely not a constant environment! As application programmers, we accept and understand the need for change, so doesn't it make good sense to recognize that files change too?

The AMS command LISTCAT is the most efficient tool available for monitoring file performance. LISTCAT will print details about entries cataloged in either the master catalog or any user catalog. The report produced by LISTCAT reveals a great deal of information about clusters and how they are performing.

Before I continue discussing LISTCATs, let's review what is stored in a catalog. Objects housed in a catalog include base clusters, data and index components, alternate indexes and paths. Examples of the information a LISTCAT tells about these objects are:

1) Creation and expiration dates
2) Security provisions
3) Statistical data regarding usage
4) Space allocations
5) Characteristics of the object (i.e., CI splits)

Does every LISTCAT look alike? No. Not only does the object itself influence the report, but so do the selected parameters. A LISTCAT can be limited to specific objects, and it can also be limited by the amount of information printed for each of the objects.

By using the appropriate parameters, you can tailor LISTCAT to:

1) List all catalog-related information contained in an entire catalog. All available information for each of these objects will be formatted to a report.

2) List all catalog-related information for a specific object. For example, you can request a LISTCAT on INV.MASTER.FILE only.

3) List a condensed version of catalog-related information contained in an entire catalog.

4) List a condensed version of catalog-related information for a specific object. For example, you can request a limited LISTCAT on INV.ACCT.EXT only.

Now, let's take a look at how to code the LISTCAT command.

```
LISTCAT    [CATALOG(name[/password])]
           [ENTRIES(entryname[/password]...]
           [entry-type]
           NAME | VOLUME | ALLOCATION | ALL]
           [NOTUSABLE]
```

CATALOG   May be abbreviated as CAT. Specifies the name of

141

the catalog to be listed. If the catalog is password protected, the valid *password* must be coded. If the CATALOG parameter is omitted, the job catalog specified in the accompanying JCL is listed. If the latter is not present, LISTCAT generates a report on the master catalog.

ENTRIES   May be abbreviated as ENT. Specifies names of the catalog entries to be listed. *entryname* is the object's name, and *password* is its related password. If you omit this parameter, all entries housed in the selected catalog are listed unless you limit your selection with the *entry-type* parameter.

entry-type   Specifies the type of entries to be listed. Valid values are:

ALTERNATEINDEX   or AIX
CLUSTER   or CL
DATA   - - - - -   (lists data components only)
INDEX   or IX (lists index components only)
SPACE   or SPC
USERCATALOG   or UCAT

If the *entry-name* parameter is omitted, all types of entries stored in the selected catalog are listed unless the selection is limited with the ENTRIES parameter.

NAME | VOLUME | ALLOCATION   ALL Specifies the type of information to be listed.

NAME   Lists only the names and types of selected entries.

VOLUME   May be abbreviated as VOL. Lists the name, owner identification, creation and expiration dates, VSAM release ID at creation time, volume serial number and device type used for physical allocation of the selected entries. Also, if the data is available, VOLUME will list the catalog recovery volume serial number, control interval number and device type. However, volume-related information is not listed for clusters, alternate indexes or paths.

ALLOCATION   May be abbreviated as ALLOC. Lists the volume as well as detailed information about the allocation of selected entries. However, this information is only available for data and index components.

ALL   Lists all fields contained in the selected entries. If the entry is password protected, this information is also listed. The default value for this parameter is NAME.

NOTUSABLE   May be abbreviated as NUS. Lists only damaged catalog entries. These entries are either data or index components.

Clearly, the parameters indicate what a wealth of information a LISTCAT can provide. It is the most useful tool we have for tuning VSAM files.

Now that you know how to code a LISTCAT command, let's interpret the output. Information produced by a LISTCAT can basically be summarized as follows:

ALLOCATION	Fields that describe space allocation for data
GROUP	and index components.
ASSOCIATIONS	Fields that identify other entries associated
GROUP	with the entry being reported on.
ATTRIBUTES	Fields that describe characteristics of the
GROUP	data and index components.
DATA SPACE	Fields that describe characteristics of the
GROUP	data space.
HISTORY	Fields that identify the entry's owner as well
GROUP	as creation and expiration dates.
PROTECTION	Fields that describe how the entry is password protected.
GROUP	word protected.
STATISTICS	Fields that provide information related to

STATISTICS GROUP   Fields that provide information related to growth and performance. These numbers and percentages indicate how much activity has occurred in the processing of data and index components.

VOLUME GROUP   Fields that identify the volume(s) on which an entry is housed.

See Table 9.1 for LISTCAT device codes.

Before I show you some examples of the output produced by LISTCAT, we need to define the terminology that appears on these reports. To simplify these explanations, I've categorized the fields according to group. Included with each group is a list of associated entry types and references to non-VSAM files. For more information on this topic, refer to Chapter 12.

ALLOCATION GROUP

Pertains to data and index components.

HI-ALLOC-RBA   The highest RBA (plus 1) within the allocated space that is available for storage.

TABLE 9-1. Device Codes

The device codes used in reports produced by LISTCAT may be translated as follows:

Code	Type
30008001	9-track tape
3010200C	3375
3010200E	3380
3040200A	3340 (35M or 70M)
30502006	2305-1
30502007	2305-2
30502009	3330-1 or 3330-2
3050200B	3350
3050200D	3330-11
30582009	3330 MSS virtual storage
30808001	7-track tape
30C02008	2314 or 2319

HI-USED-RBA	The highest RBA (plus 1) within the allocated space that actually contains data.
SPACE-PRI	Specifies in units (see SPACE-TYPE) how much primary space is allocated to the data or index component at definition time.
SPACE-SEC	Specifies in units (see SPACE-TYPE) how much secondary space is allocated to the data or index component. This space will be used once the primary allocation is exceeded.
SPACE-TYPE	Indicates the type of unit used for space allocations. Valid types are BLOCK, CYLINDER, RECORD and TRACK.

ASSOCIATIONS GROUP

Pertains to data and index components, alternate indexes, paths and clusters.

In this group, pointers are made to related catalog entries. For example, an alternate index entry will point to the associated path. Abbreviations used to describe these relationships are:

AIX	Alternate index entry
CLUSTER	Cluster entry
DATA	Data entry
INDEX	Index entry
NON-VSAM	A non-VSAM file entry
PATH	Path entry
UCAT	User catalog entry

ATTRIBUTES GROUP

Pertains to data and index components, alternate indexes and paths.

| AVGLRECL | Indicates the average length of records. |
| AXRKP | Applies only to an AI. This is the AI's relative key position. The value given for AXRKP specifies where the alternate-key field begins in relation to the start of the cluster's data record. |

BUFSPACE	The minimum buffer space available in virtual storage.
CIFORMAT	Applies only to SAM files managed under VSAM.
CI/CA	Specifies the number of control intervals contained in each control area.
CISIZE	Indicates control interval size in terms of bytes.
ERASE	When a record is deleted, binary zeros will be moved to the record's fields. This in effect says that the record has been erased.
EXCPEXIT	Specifies name of an exception exit routine.
EXP-DEFINE	Applies only to SAM files managed under VSAM.
IMBED	An option which may be selected during the DEFINE command. Stores the sequence-set index record with its associated data control area.
IMP-DEFINE	Applies only to SAM files managed under VSAM.
INH-UPDATE	Indicates that the data component cannot be updated.
INDEXED	KSDS file identifier.
KEYLEN	Specifies the key field's length.
MAXLRECL	Indicates the maximum length of records.
MAXRECS	Applies only to an RRDS. The value given for this field is the highest relative-record number contained in the file.
NOALLOC	Space is not allocated to the file.
NOCIFORMAT	Applies only to SAM files managed under VSAM.
NOERASE	When a record is deleted, the record's fields remain intact. This in effect says that the record has not been erased.
NOIMBED	The sequence-set index record is not stored with its associated data control area.
NONINDEXED	ESDS file identifier.
NONSPANNED	Records cannot span CIs.

NONUNIQKEY	Applies only to an AI. Allows more than one data record to contain the same alternate-key value.
NOREPLICAT	Specifies that index records are not to be replicated.
NOREUSE	File cannot be reused.
NOTUSABLE	Catalog entry is not usable.
NOUPDATE	Applies only to a path. When the latter is opened for processing, its associated cluster and AI are opened, but the cluster's upgrade set is not opened.
NOUPGRADE	Applies only to an AI. The latter is not upgraded unless it's opened and used for accessing the cluster's data records.
NOWRITECHK	Indicates that write operations are not verified for media recording accuracy.
NUMBERED	RRDS file identifier.
ORDERED	Specifies that volume usage for space allocation is to occur in the order such volumes were coded for by the DEFINE command.
RECFORMAT	Applies only to SAM files managed under VSAM.
RECOVERY	Results in a temporary CLOSE after each CA is loaded. This option eliminates having to reload the entire file if a serious error occurs during the loading process.
RECORDS/CI	Applies only to an RRDS. Specifies the number of slots contained in a CI.
RECVABLE	Applies only to a recoverable catalog. This option affords each of the catalog's DASD volumes with a catalog recovery area.
REPLICATE	Option which results in index records being duplicated around a track of the index's volume.
REUSE	Indicates the file can be reused.
RKP	*Relative key position.* Positional indicator specifying the key field's starting position.

	RKP is offset from the start of the logical record.
SAMDATASET	Applies only to SAM files managed under VSAM.
SAMLRECL	Applies only to SAM files managed under VSAM.
SHROPTNS	Codes established with the DEFINE command specifying the type of sharing permitted. Both cross-region and cross-system share options are available. The first code specified is cross-region and the second is cross-system.
SPANNED	Indicates that data records can be longer than the CI length. Also, data records can cross CI boundaries.
SPEED	Results in a CLOSE not being issued until the file is loaded. This option requires having to reload the entire file if a serious error occurs during the loading process.
SUBALLOC	Allows more than one cluster or AI to share the same data space.
TEMP-EXP	Indicates that the TEMPORARY option was used when the file was exported.
UNIQUE	Allows only one cluster or AI to use data space.
UNIQUEKEY	Applies only to an AI. Each data record must have a unique alternate key.
UNORDERED	Allows usage of DASD volumes in any order regardless of how they are specified during the DEFINE command.
UPDATE	Opens the upgrade set's AIs when the path is opened.
UPGRADE	Opens the AI when the AI's base cluster is opened.
VSAMDATSET	VSAM ESDS file indicator.
WRITECHECK	Indicates that write operations are verified.

DATA SPACE GROUP.

Pertains to data space.

ATTRIBUTES   Describes characteristics of data space.
  AUTOMATIC   Indicates data space was created by a
    secondary allocation operation.
  CLASS   Specifies the class of space on the DASD
    volume.
  EXPLICIT   Indicates data space was explicitly created.
  MASTERCAT   Data space contains the master catalog.
  SUBALLOC   Data space may contain several clusters.
  USERCAT   Data space contains a user catalog.
  UNIQUE   Data space contains only one component
    (may be data or index).

DATASET DIRECTORY   Lists those files that already are or can
  be stored in the data space.
  ATTRIBUTES   Describe the relationship between the
    named file and the data space.

  • CANDIDATE—Volume is a candidate for
    storing the file.
  • (NULL)—File is stored in the data space.

DSN   Name of the stored object.
EXTENTS   Number of files suballocated extents within the data
  space.

DATASETS   Number of VSAM files stored in the data space.
EXTENT-DESCRIPTOR   Describes the data space extent.

  BEG-BLOCK   Applies to FBA devices only. Specifies in
    decimal the device address of the extents.
  BEG-COHH   Gives the device address of the extent.
  BLOCKS-TOTAL   Applies to FBA devices only. Spec-
    ifies in decimal format the total number of
    blocks allocated to the data space.
  BLOCKS-USED   Applies to FBA devices only. Specifies
    in decimal format the total number of blocks
    allocated to files and catalogs.

SPACE-MAP   For CKD devices, specifies in hexadecimal which
  tracks are used and which tracks are free in the extent.

SPACE-MAP   For FBA devices, specifies in hexadecimal which blocks are used and which blocks are free in the extent.

TRACKS-TOTAL   Specifies in decimal the total number of tracks allocated to the data space.

TRACKS-USED   Specifies in decimal the total number of tracks allocated to files and catalogs.

EXTENTS   The number of file suballocated extents contained in the data space.

FORMAT-1-LABEL   Identifies the DASD volume's Format-1 label used for the data space.

> BLOCK   Applies to FBA devices only. Specifies in decimal the address of the Format-1 label in the VTOC.
>
> CCHHR   The device address of the Format-1 label in the VTOC.
>
> TIMESTAMP   The time-of-day clock value that the data space was allocated.
>
> SEC-ALLOCEN   Specifies the amount of space to be allocated whenever data space is extended. The amount of space is given in unit indicators; refer to TYPE for the latter.
>
> TYPE   Describes for allocation purposes the unit of space. Available type indicators are BLOCK, CYLINDER, and TRACK.

HISTORY GROUP

Pertains to data and index components, alternate indexes, paths and clusters.

entryname   Identifies the name of the cataloged object.

HISTORY   The following historical data is listed under this subheading.

> CREATION   Specifies in Julian date format when the entry was created.
>
> EXPIRATION   Specifies in Julian date format when the entry can be deleted without using the DELETE command's PURGE parameter.

OWNER-IDENT   Identifies the owner of the object.
RCVY-CI   Applies only to entries in a recoverable
catalog. Contains the CI number in the catalog
recovery area where a duplicate of the entry can
be found.
RCVY-DEVI   Applies only to entries in a recoverable
catalog. Contains the recovery volume's serial
number.
RELEASE   Specifies the VSAM release under which the
entry was created.

PROTECTION GROUP

Pertains to data and index components, alternate indexes,
paths and clusters.

NULL   Indicates that the defined object has no passwords.
SUPP   Indicates that the master password for neither the
catalog nor the defined object is specified. Protection-
related information cannot be listed.
ATTEMPTS   Specifies the number of times a console operator
can attempt to enter the correct password. ATTEMPTS
may have a value of 0 through 7.
CODE   Identifies to the console operator which object requires
a password. If CODE is used, the actual file-ID is not
revealed during the password prompting process.
CONTROLPW   The CI password.
MASTERPW   The master password.
REALPW   The read-only password.
UPDATEPW   The update password.
USAR   Exhibits the contents of the user-security-authorization
record.
USVR   Exhibits the name of the user-written program that can
verify authorization access to the entry.

STATISTICS GROUP

Pertains to data and index components.

FREESPACE-%CI   Percentage of free space in a CI. This volume is the one requested by the user; the actual amount of free space may be different.

FREESPACE-%CI   Percentage of CIs to be left free in a CA. This value is the one requested by the user; the actual number might be different.

FREESPC-BYTES   For the data component of a KSDS or RRDS, represents the actual number of bytes of unused CAs in the allocated space. For the data component of an ESDS, represents the actual number of bytes of unused CIs at the end of the file. For the index component, represents the actual number of bytes of unused CIs at the end of the component.

INDEX   Information displayed under this category complies only to an index component.

ENTRIES/SECT   Specifies the desired number of entries in each section of entries in an index record.

HI-LEVEL-RBA   The RBA of the highest-level index record.

LEVELS   Specifies the number of record levels in the index.

SEQ-SET-REA   Specifies in decimal the field that contains the RBA of the first sequence-set record.

SYSTEM-TIMESTAMP   The time-of-day clock value that the component was last closed.

The following fields are updated only when the file is closed.

EXCPS   EXCP macro instructions issued by VSAM against the component. EXCP is an acronym for execute channel program.

EXTENTS   Specifies the component's extents.

REC-DELETED   The number of records that have been deleted from the component.

REC-INSERTED   The number of records that have been inserted into the component. These records have not been added to the end of file.

REC-RETRIEVED   The number of records that have been
retrieved from the component.

REC-TOTAL   For a KSDS or ESDS, the total number of records
actually in the component. For an RRDS, the total
number of slots that have been formatted in the
component.

REC-UPDATED   The total number of records that have been
updated and rewritten. Deleted records are not included
in this total.

SPLITS-CA   Control-area splits.

SPLITS-CI   Control-interval splits.

VOLUMES GROUP

Pertains to data components and index components.

BLOCKS/CA   Applies to FBA devices only. Specifies in decimal
the number of blocks that comprise a CA.

BLKS/MIH-CA   Applies to FBA devices only. Specifies in decimal the number of blocks that can be written to a
volume's minimum CA unit.

DEVTYPE   The volume's device type.

EXTENT-NUMBER   Specifies the number of allocated extents.

EXTENT-TYPE   Identifies the type of extents. Valid values are:

00 Contiguous extents.
40 May be contiguous but are not preformatted.
80 A sequence set occupies a track adjacent to a CA.

EXTENTS   Information related to the physical and
relative-byte addresses of each extent.

BLOCKS   Applies to FBA devices only. Specifies in decimal the number of blocks in the extent.

HIGH-BLOCK   Applies to FBA devices only. Identifies
the device address where the extent ends.

HIGH-CCHH   Applies to CKD devices only. Identifies
the device address where the extent ends.

HIGH-RBA   Specifies in decimal the RBA where the
extent ends.

LOCK-BLOCK   Applies to FBA devices only. Identifies the device address where the extent begins.

LOW-CCHH   Applies to CKD devices only. Identifies the device address where the extent begins.

LOW-RBA   Specifies in decimal the RBA where the extent begins.

TRACKS   The total number of tracks in the extent.

HIGH-KEY   Applies only to KSDS with the KEYRANGE attribute. Specifies the highest hexadecimal value allowed in the key field of a record contained in the key range.

HI-KEY-RBA   Applies to a KSDS only. Specifies in decimal format the RBA of the CI that contains the record with the highest key in the file or key range.

LOW-KEY   Applies only to a KSDS with the KEYRANGE attribute. Specifies the lowest hexadecimal value allowed in the key field of a record contained in the key range.

PHYRECSA/TRK   The number of physical records that can be written on a track. The size of these records is specified by the PHYREC-SIZE field.

PHYREC-SIZE   The number of physical bytes used for a record.

HI-ALLOC-RBA   The highest RBA (plus 1) available within allocated space for storage purposes.

HI-USED-RBA   For the data component of a KSDS or RRDS, specifies the highest RBA of a CA (plus 1) that contains data. For the data component of an ESDS, specifies the highest RBA of CI (plus 1) that contains data. For an index component, specifies the highest RBA of a CI (plus 1) that contains index records.

TRACKS/CA   The number of tracks that comprise a CA.

VOLFLAG   Identifies how the volume is used. Valid values are:

CANDIDATE   A candidate for storing the component but has no space allocated for the object.

OVERFLOW   An overflow volume on which data records in a key range are stored. The keyrange begins on a PRIME volume.

PRIME First volume on which data records in a key range are stored.

VOLSER Volume serial identifier.

The following fields are used to describe the space VSAM uses on the volume.

volume serial number Identifies the cataloged volume entry.

BLKS/MAX-CA Applies to FBA devices only. Specifies in decimal format the number of blocks in the largest CA on the volume.

BLKS/MIN-CA Applies to FBA devices only. Specifies in decimal format the number of blocks in a minimum CA unit.

BLOCKS/VOL Applies to FBA devices only. Specifies in decimal format the number of available blocks on the volume. Alternate blocks reserved for error recovery are not included.

BYTES/TRK The number of bytes on each track available for VSAM usage. Alternate track cylinders are included.

CYLS/VOL The number of cylinders on each volume available for VSAM usage. Alternate track cylinders are included.

DATASETS-ON-VOL The number of VSAM clusters that reside on the volume. Such clusters may exist in whole or in part.

DATASPCS-ON-VOL The number of VSAM data spaces on the volume.

DEVTYPE A volume's device type.

MAX-PHYREC-SZ Specifies the size of the largest physical record that can be written.

MAX-EXT/ALLOC Specifies the maximum number of extents that can be suballocated for a single file.

TRKS/CYL The number of tracks in each cylinder.

VOLUME-TIMESTAMP The time-of-day clock value that the volume's contents were last changed.

Following are the outputs produced by various options offered by the LISTCAT command.

```
/ / JOB LISTCAT1
/ / EXEC IDCAMS,SIZE = AUTO
   LISTCAT -
      CATALOG(VSAM.BATCH.ONE.UCAT        BTCHVS1)
/*
/&
```

LISTCAT output when no parameters are specified

```
             LISTING FROM CATALOG -- VSAM.BATCH.ONE.UCAT
       DATA ------- INVT.MASTER.FILE.DATA

       INDEX ------ INVT.MASTER.FILE.INDEX

    CLUSTER ------- INVT.TRAN.FILE

       DATA ------- INVT.TRAN.FILE.DATA

    CLUSTER ------- MLA.LLG1.FILE

       DATA ------- MLA.LLG1.DATA

       INDEX ------ MLA.LLG1.INDEX

    CLUSTER ------- MLA.PART1.FILE

       DATA ------- MLA.PART1.DATA

       INDEX ------ MLA.PART1.INDEX

    CLUSTER ------- NVSM.F676.ACTLIMIT

       DATA ------- NVSM.F676.ACTLIMIT.DATA

       INDEX ------ NVSM.F676.ACTLIMIT.INDEX

    CLUSTER ------- NVSM.F676.DDAKEYEX

       DATA ------- NVSM.F676.DDAKEYEX.DATA

       INDEX ------ NVSM.F676.DDAKEYEX.INDEX

    CLUSTER ------- OLD.ITST.DDA.TRANS

       DATA ------- OLD.ITST.DDA.TRANS.DATA

       INDEX ------ OLD.ITST.DDA.TRANS.INDEX

    CLUSTER ------- OLD.ITST.TDA.TRANS
```

156

OUTPUT 9-1. Continued.

```
DATA ------- OLD.ITST.TDA.TRANS.DATA
INDEX ------ OLD.ITST.TDA.TRANS.INDEX
CLUSTER ------- OLDT.ITS.DDA.TRANS
DATA ------- OLDT.ITS.DDA.TRANS.DATA
```

OUTPUT 9-2.

```
         LISTING FROM CATALOG -- VSAM.BATCH.ONE.UCAT
   INDEX ------ VSAM.CATALOG.BASE.INDEX.RECORD
VOLUME -------- 335003
VOLUME -------- 335005
VOLUME -------- 335011
VOLUME -------- 335012
VOLUME -------- 335013
VOLUME -------- 335020
VOLUME -------- 335021
VOLUME -------- 335022
```

OUTPUT 9-3.

```
      LISTING FROM CATALOG -- VSAM.BATCH.ONE.UCAT

   THE NUMBER OF ENTRIES PROCESSED WAS:
                 AIX ------------------0
                 CLUSTER --------------53
                 DATA -----------------53
                 INDEX ----------------39
                 NONVSAM --------------0
                 PATH -----------------0
                 SPACE ----------------8
                 USERCATALOG ----------0
                 TOTAL ---------------153

   THE NUMBER OF PROTECTED ENTRIES SUPPRESSED WAS 0

IDC0001I FUNCTION COMPLETED, HIGHEST CONDITION CODE WAS 0
```

```
/ / JOB LISTCAT2
/ / EXEC IDCAMS,SIZE = AUTO
   LISTCAT -
      VOLUME
/*
/&
```

LISTCAT VOLUME output

```
              LISTING FROM CATALOG -- VSAM.MASTER.CATALOG

CLUSTER ------- CICS.VS.TEMP.STORAGE
      HISTORY
            OWNER-IDENT------- (NULL)      CREATION----------86.307
            RELEASE---------------2        EXPIRATION--------00.000

    DATA ------- CICS.VS.TEMP.STORAGE.DATA
      HISTORY
            OWNER-IDENT------- (NULL)      CREATION----------86.307
            RELEASE---------------2        EXPIRATION--------00.000
      VOLUMES
            VOLSER-----------335009        DEVTYPE------X'3010200B'

VOLUME -------- DOSRES
      HISTORY
            RELEASE---------------2
      VOLUMES
            VOLSER-----------DOSRES        DEVTYPE------X'3010200B'

USERCATALOG --- VSAM.BATCH.ONE.UCAT
      HISTORY
            RELEASE---------------2
      VOLUMES
            VOLSER-----------335011        DEVTYPE------X'3010200B'

CLUSTER ------- VSAM.MASTER.CATALOG
      HISTORY
            OWNER-IDENT------- (NULL)      CREATION----------84.056
            RELEASE---------------2        EXPIRATION--------00.000

    DATA ------- VSAM.CATALOG.BASE.DATA.RECORD
      HISTORY
            OWNER-IDENT------- (NULL)      CREATION----------84.056
            RELEASE----------------2       EXPIRATION--------00.000
      VOLUMES
            VOLSER-----------DOSRES        DEVTYPE------X'3010200B'

    INDEX ------ VSAM.CATALOG.BASE.INDEX.RECORD
      HISTORY
            OWNER-IDENT------- (NULL)      CREATION----------84.056
            RELEASE---------------2        EXPIRATION--------00.000
```

OUTPUT 9-4. Continued.

```
VOLUMES
  VOLSER-----------DOSRES        DEVTYPE------X'3010200B'
USERCATALOG --- VSAM.ONL.TEST.UCAT
  HISTORY
    RELEASE----------------2
  VOLUMES
    VOLSER-----------335029      DEVTYPE------X'3010200B'
```

OUTPUT 9-5.

```
        LISTING FROM CATALOG -- VSAM.MASTER.CATALOG

USERCATALOG --- VSAM.ONLINE.UCAT
  HISTORY
    RELEASE----------------2
  VOLUMES
    VOLSER-----------335010      DEVTYPE------X'3010200B'
VOLUME -------- 335009
  HISTORY
    RELEASE----------------2
  VOLUMES
    VOLSER-----------335009      DEVTYPE------X'3010200B'
```

OUTPUT 9-6.

```
      LISTING FROM CATALOG -- VSAM.MASTER.CATALOG

THE NUMBER OF ENTRIES PROCESSED WAS:
    AIX --------------------0
    CLUSTER ----------------2
    DATA -------------------2
    INDEX ------------------1
    NONVSAM ----------------0
    PATH -------------------0
    SPACE ------------------2
    USERCATALOG ------------3
    TOTAL ------------------10

THE NUMBER OF PROTECTED ENTRIES SUPPRESSED WAS 0
IDC0001I FUNCTION COMPLETED, HIGHEST CONDITION CODE WAS 0
```

```
// JOB LISTCAT3
// EXEC IDCAMS,SIZE = AUTO
    LISTCAT -
        SPACE -
        ALL -
            CATALOG(VSAM.BATCH.ONE.UCAT        BTCHVS1)
/*
/&
```

LISTCAT SPACE ALL output

LISTING FROM CATALOG -

```
VOLUME -------- 335003
        HISTORY
            RELEASE----------------2
        CHARACTERISTICS
            BYTES/TRK--------------0        DEVTYPE---------.........
            TRKS/CYL---------------0        VOLUME-TIMESTAMP:
            CYLS/VOL---------------0            X'9AE3CE0643EAC000'
        DATASPACE
            DATASETS---------------8        FORMAT-1-LABEL:
            EXTENTS----------------1        CCHHR------X'022A000116'
            SEC-ALLOC--------------0        TIMESTAMP
            TYPE------------CYLINDER            X'9AE3CE0643EAC000'
            CLASS-----------------0
            EXTENT-DESCRIPTOR:
            TRACKS-TOTAL--------3370        BEG-CCHH-----X'00010000'
            TRACKS-USED----------158
            DATASET-DIRECTORY:
                DSN----CAP.BATCH.DATA
                DSN----CAP.BATCH.INDEX
                DSN----CPBT.SYSTEM.CTRL.FILE.DATA
                DSN----CPBT.SYSTEM.CTRL.FILE.INDEX
                DSN----OLDT.ITS.DDA.TRANS.DATA
                DSN----OLDT.ITS.DDA.TRANS.INDEX
                DSN----OLDT.ITS.TDA.TRANS.DATA
                DSN----OLDT.ITS.TDA.TRANS.INDEX

VOLUME -------- 335005
        HISTORY
            RELEASE----------------2
        CHARACTERISTICS
            BYTES/TRK--------------0        DEVTYPE---------.........
            TRKS/CYL---------------0        VOLUME-TIMESTAMP:
            CYLS/VOL---------------0            X'9AE3CD335E1FA000'
        DATASPACE
            DATASETS--------------30        FORMAT-1-LABEL:
            EXTENTS----------------1        CCHHR------X'022A000105'
            SEC-ALLOC--------------0        TIMESTAMP
            TYPE------------CYLINDER            X'9AE3CD01257DA000'
            CLASS-----------------0
            EXTENT-DESCRIPTOR:
            TRACKS-TOTAL--------5280        BEG-CCHH-----X'00290000'

            TRACKS-USED---------4673
            DATASET-DIRECTORY:
                DSN----FCS.VSAM.GLF100.DATA
                DSN----FCS.VSAM.GLF100.INDEX
                DSN----NVSM.F676.DDAKEYEX.DATA
                DSN----NVSM.F676.DDAKEYEX.INDEX
```

160

```
MAX-PHYREC-SZ----------0      DATASETS-ON-VOL-------30
MAX-EXT/ALLOC----------5       DATASPCS-ON-VOL--------1

ATTRIBUTES:
SUBALLOC
EXPLICIT


SPACE-MAP----------00FD186E04089AFD079E

ATTRIBUTES--------(NULL)      EXTENTS----------------1
ATTRIBUTES--------(NULL)      EXTENTS----------------1
ATTRIBUTES--------(NULL)      EXTENTS----------------1
ATTRIBUTES--------(NULL)      EXTENTS----------------1
ATTRIBUTES--------(NULL)      EXTENTS----------------1
ATTRIBUTES--------(NULL)      EXTENTS----------------1
ATTRIBUTES--------(NULL)      EXTENTS----------------1
ATTRIBUTES--------(NULL)      EXTENTS----------------1



MAX-PHYREC-SZ----------0      DATASETS-ON-VOL-------61
MAX-EXT/ALLOC----------5       DATASPCS-ON-VOL--------2

ATTRIBUTES:
SUBALLOC
EXPLICIT



SPACE-MAP----------1F030B0FFD0BF43CFD012CB4FD02D41503
                   1EFD0276F91401031B6315

ATTRIBUTES--------(NULL)      EXTENTS----------------1
ATTRIBUTES--------(NULL)      EXTENTS----------------1
ATTRIBUTES--------(NULL)      EXTENTS----------------1
ATTRIBUTES--------(NULL)      EXTENTS----------------1
```

```
DSN----FCS.VSAM.GLF200.INDEX
DSN----OLD.ITST.DDA.TRANS.DATA
DSN----OLD.ITST.DDA.TRANS.INDEX
DSN----OLD.ITST.TDA.TRANS.DATA
DSN----OLD.ITST.TDA.TRANS.INDEX
DSN----ACH.ACH030.FISXHD.DATA
DSN----FCST.VSAM.GLF470.DATA
DSN----OLDT.TDAC.SORTED.TRANS.DATA
DSN----OLDT.TDAC.SORTED.TRANS.INDEX
DSN----CAP.ACCUM.TRAN.DATA
DSN----ONE.BANK.CONTROL.DATA
DSN----ONE.BANK.CONTROL.INDEX
DSN----FCST.VSAM.GLF470.INDEX
DSN----NVSM.F676.ACTLIMIT.DATA
DSN----NVSM.F676.ACTLIMIT.INDEX
DSN----ACH.ACH440.FISXDG.DATA
DSN----INVT.MASTER.FILE.DATA
DSN----INVT.MASTER.FILE.INDEX
DSN----INVT.TRAN.FILE.DATA
DSN----CPBT.CRDHLDR.FILE.DATA
DSN----CPBT.CRDHLDR.FILE.INDEX
DSN----DDI.ORG.CTL.MASTER.DATA
DSN----DDI.ORG.CTL.MASTER.INDEX
DSN----DDS.WORKFILE.SYSD.DFD86287.T9BACAA3.T8C17910
DSN----FCST.VSAM.GLF410.DATA
DSN----FCST.VSAM.GLF410.INDEX
DATASPACE
    DATASETS---------------1          FORMAT-1-LABEL:
    EXTENTS----------------1          CCHHR------X'022A000108'
    SEC-ALLOC--------------0          TIMESTAMP
    TYPE-----------CYLINDER                X'9AE3CD335E1FA000'
    CLASS------------------0
    EXTENT-DESCRIPTOR:
    TRACKS-TOTAL--------7300           BEG-CCHH-----X'01260000'
    TRACKS-USED---------450
    DATASET-DIRECTORY:
        DSN----FCS.VSAM.GLF200.DATA

VOLUME -------- 335011
    HISTORY
        RELEASE---------------2
    CHARACTERISTICS
        BYTES/TRK-------------0        DEVTYPE---------........
        TRKS/CYL-------------0         VOLUME-TIMESTAMP:
        CYLS/VOL-------------0             X'9AE3CC98EEB79000'
    DATASPACE
        DATASETS-------------1         FORMAT-1-LABEL:
        EXTENTS--------------1         CCHHR------X'022A000106'
```

```
ATTRIBUTES--------(NULL)        EXTENTS-----------------1
ATTRIBUTES--------(NULL)        EXTENTS-----------------1
ATTRIBUTES--------(NULL)        EXTENTS-----------------1
ATTRIBUTES--------(NULL)        EXTENTS-----------------1
ATTRIBUTES--------(NULL)        EXTENTS-----------------1
ATTRIBUTES--------(NULL)        EXTENTS-----------------1
ATTRIBUTES--------(NULL)        EXTENTS-----------------1
ATTRIBUTES--------(NULL)        EXTENTS-----------------1
ATTRIBUTES--------(NULL)        EXTENTS-----------------1
ATTRIBUTES--------(NULL)        EXTENTS-----------------1
ATTRIBUTES--------(NULL)        EXTENTS-----------------1
ATTRIBUTES--------(NULL)        EXTENTS-----------------1
ATTRIBUTES--------(NULL)        EXTENTS-----------------1
ATTRIBUTES--------(NULL)        EXTENTS-----------------1
ATTRIBUTES--------(NULL)        EXTENTS-----------------1
ATTRIBUTES--------(NULL)        EXTENTS-----------------1
ATTRIBUTES--------(NULL)        EXTENTS-----------------2
ATTRIBUTES--------(NULL)        EXTENTS-----------------1
ATTRIBUTES--------(NULL)        EXTENTS-----------------1
ATTRIBUTES--------(NULL)        EXTENTS-----------------1
ATTRIBUTES--------(NULL)        EXTENTS-----------------1
ATTRIBUTES--------(NULL)        EXTENTS-----------------1
ATTRIBUTES--------(NULL)        EXTENTS-----------------1
ATTRIBUTES--------(NULL)        EXTENTS-----------------1
ATTRIBUTES--------(NULL)        EXTENTS-----------------1
```

```
ATTRIBUTES:
SUBALLOC
EXPLICIT
```

```
SPACE-MAP-----------00FD19AAFD01C2FD030C
```

```
ATTRIBUTES--------(NULL)        EXTENTS-----------------1
```

```
MAX-PHYREC-SZ----------0         DATASETS-ON-VOL-------66
MAX-EXT/ALLOC----------5         DATASPCS-ON-VOL--------3
```

```
ATTRIBUTES:
SUBALLOC
```

```
        SEC-ALLOC-------------0        TIMESTAMP
        TYPE---------------TRACK           X'9AE3CAC289FC3000'
        CLASS----------------0
        EXTENT-DESCRIPTOR:
        TRACKS-TOTAL----------90       BEG-CCHH-----X'00010000'
        TRACKS-USED-----------90
        DATASET-DIRECTORY:
          DSN----VSAM.BATCH.ONE.UCAT
DATASPACE
        DATASETS--------------2        FORMAT-1-LABEL:
        EXTENTS---------------1        CCHHR------X'022A000107'
        SEC-ALLOC-------------0        TIMESTAMP
        TYPE-----------CYLINDER            X'9AE3CC64DF6D2000'
        CLASS----------------0
        EXTENT-DESCRIPTOR:
        TRACKS-TOTAL-------3280         BEG-CCHH-----X'00040000'
        TRACKS-USED--------903
        DATASET-DIRECTORY:
          DSN----VSAM.BATCH.ONE.UCAT
          DSN----CPBT.CUSTOMER.FILE.DATA
DATASPACE
        DATASETS--------------6        FORMAT-1-LABEL:
        EXTENTS---------------1        CCHHR------X'022A000108'
        SEC-ALLOC-------------0        TIMESTAMP
        TYPE-----------CYLINDER            X'9AE3CC98EEB79000'
        CLASS----------------0
        EXTENT-DESCRIPTOR:
        TRACKS-TOTAL-------1800         BEG-CCHH-----X'01400000'
        TRACKS-USED--------946
        DATASET-DIRECTORY:
          DSN----VSAM.BATCH.ONE.UCAT
          DSN----FCS.VSAM.GLF200.DATA
          DSN----ACH.ACH410.FISXCU.DATA
          DSN----CPBT.CUSTOMER.FILE.INDEX
          DSN----SAV.ORGAN.MASTER.FILE.DATA
          DSN----SAV.ORGAN.MASTER.FILE.INDEX
VOLUME -------- 335012
    HISTORY
        RELEASE---------------2
    CHARACTERISTICS
        BYTES/TRK-------------0        DEVTYPE---------........
        TRKS/CYL-------------0         VOLUME-TIMESTAMP:
        CYLS/VOL-------------0             X'9AE3CCCBC8E4F000'
    DATASPACE
        DATASETS------------10         FORMAT-1-LABEL:
        EXTENTS--------------1         CCHHR------X'0000001904'
        SEC-ALLOC-----------0          TIMESTAMP
```

164

- VSAM.BATCH.ONE.UCAT

OUTPUT 9-9.

EXPLICIT
USERCAT

SPACE-MAP----------5A

ATTRIBUTES--------(NULL)   EXTENTS----------------3
ATTRIBUTES:
SUBALLOC
EXPLICIT
USERCAT

SPACE-MAP----------FD0384FD1C7E0353

ATTRIBUTES--------(NULL)   EXTENTS--------------------1
ATTRIBUTES--------(NULL)   EXTENTS--------------------1

ATTRIBUTES:
SUBALLOC
EXPLICIT
USERCAT

SPACE-MAP----------21020D0CFD0384FD0348

ATTRIBUTES--------(NULL)   EXTENTS----------------4
ATTRIBUTES--------(NULL)   EXTENTS----------------1
ATTRIBUTES--------(NULL)   EXTENTS----------------1
ATTRIBUTES--------(NULL)   EXTENTS----------------1
ATTRIBUTES--------(NULL)   EXTENTS----------------1
ATTRIBUTES--------(NULL)   EXTENTS----------------1

MAX-PHYREC-SZ----------0   DATASETS-ON-VOL-------62
MAX-EXT/ALLOC----------5   DATASPCS-ON-VOL--------1

ATTRIBUTES:
SUBALLOC
EXPLICIT

165

```
      TYPE------------CYLINDER              X'9AE3CCCBC8E4F000'
      CLASS-------------------0
      EXTENT-DESCRIPTOR:
      TRACKS-TOTAL--------8280             BEG-CCHH-----X'00020000'

      TRACKS-USED---------1869
      DATASET-DIRECTORY:
        DSN----ACH.ACH400.FISXCT.DATA
        DSN----ACH.ACH420.FISXET.DATA
        DSN----ACH.ACH450.FISKEY.DATA
        DSN----CPBT.MERCHANT.FILE.DATA
        DSN----CPBT.MERCHANT.FILE.INDEX
        DSN----SAV.ACCOUNT.MASTER.FILE.DATA
        DSN----SAV.ACCOUNT.MASTER.FILE.INDEX
        DSN----MLA.LLG1.INDEX
        DSN----MLA.PART1.DATA
        DSN----MLA.PART1.INDEX

VOLUME -------- 335013
      HISTORY
        RELEASE----------------2
      CHARACTERISTICS
        BYTES/TRK--------------0             DEVTYPE---------........
        TRKS/CYL---------------0             VOLUME-TIMESTAMP:
        CYLS/VOL---------------0               X'9AE3CDD851B59000'
      DATASPACE
        DATASETS--------------5              FORMAT-1-LABEL:
        EXTENTS---------------1              CCHHR------X'022A000109'
        SEC-ALLOC-------------0              TIMESTAMP
        TYPE------------CYLINDER               X'9AE3CDD851B59000'
        CLASS-------------------0
      EXTENT-DESCRIPTOR:
        TRACKS-TOTAL--------3720             BEG-CCHH-----X'004C0000'
        TRACKS-USED---------2190
      DATASET-DIRECTORY:
        DSN---DOS.WORKFILE.SYSD.DFD86176.T9B2177E.TB0120B0
        DSN---CPT.INTEREST.CHAIN.FILE.DATA
        DSN---CPT.INTEREST.CHAIN.FILE.INDEX
        DSN---DOS.WORKFILE.SYSD.DFD86192.T9B356DD.T529D400
        DSN---MLA.LLG1.DATA

VOLUME -------- 335020
      HISTORY
        RELEASE---------------2
      CHARACTERISTICS
        BYTES/TRK-------------0              DEVTYPE---------........
        TRKS/CYL-------------0               VOLUME-TIMESTAMP:
        CYLS/VOL------------0                  X'9AE3CE36E0921000'
```

- VSAM.BATCH.ONE.UCAT

SPACE-MAP----------00FD122AB4 3CB4B9040C0504FD050CFD05
                   DC

```
ATTRIBUTES--------(NULL)        EXTENTS---------------1
ATTRIBUTES--------(NULL)        EXTENTS---------------1
ATTRIBUTES--------(NULL)        EXTENTS---------------1
ATTRIBUTES--------(NULL)        EXTENTS---------------1
ATTRIBUTES--------(NULL)        EXTENTS---------------1
ATTRIBUTES--------(NULL)        EXTENTS---------------1
ATTRIBUTES--------(NULL)        EXTENTS---------------1
ATTRIBUTES--------(NULL)        EXTENTS---------------1
ATTRIBUTES--------(NULL)        EXTENTS---------------1
ATTRIBUTES--------(NULL)        EXTENTS---------------1
```

```
MAX-PHYREC-SZ-----------0       DATASETS-ON-VOL-------27
MAX-EXT/ALLOC----------5         DATASPCS-ON-VOL--------1
```

ATTRIBUTES:
SUBALLOC
EXPLICIT

SPACE-MAP-----------0E10FD070878FD01 78FD05 72

```
ATTRIBUTES--------(NULL)        EXTENTS---------------1
ATTRIBUTES--------(NULL)        EXTENTS---------------1
ATTRIBUTES--------(NULL)        EXTENTS---------------1
ATTRIBUTES--------(NULL)        EXTENTS---------------1
ATTRIBUTES--------(NULL)        EXTENTS---------------1
```

```
MAX-PHYREC-SZ-----------0       DATASETS-ON-VOL-------27
MAX-EXT/ALLOC----------5         DATASPCS-ON-VOL--------1
```

167

```
      DATASPACE
          DATASETS---------------3          FORMAT-1-LABEL:
          EXTENTS----------------1          CCHHR------X'0000001904'
          SEC-ALLOC--------------0          TIMESTAMP
          TYPE------------CYLINDER              X'9AE3CE36E0921000'
          CLASS-----------------0
          EXTENT-DESCRIPTOR:
          TRACKS-TOTAL-------12120          BEG-CCHH-----X'00970000'
          TRACKS-USED--------7501
          DATASET-DIRECTORY:
             DSN----ACH.ACH430.FISDPX.DATA
             DSN----CPT.REPORT.TRANS.FILE.DATA
             DSN----CPT.REPORT.TRANS.FILE.INDEX

VOLUME -------- 335021
      HISTORY
          RELEASE----------------2
      CHARACTERISTICS
          BYTES/TRK--------------0          DEVTYPE---------........
          TRKS/CYL---------------0          VOLUME-TIMESTAMP:
          CYLS/VOL---------------0              X'9AE3CD6FE5D8B000'
      DATASPACE
          DATASETS---------------7          FORMAT-1-LABEL:
          EXTENTS----------------1          CCHHR------X'0000001903'
          SEC-ALLOC--------------0          TIMESTAMP
          TYPE------------CYLINDER              X'9AE3CD6FE5D8B000'
          CLASS-----------------0
          EXTENT-DESCRIPTOR:
          TRACKS-TOTAL-------16620          BEG-CCHH-----X'00010000'
          TRACKS-USED--------255
          DATASET-DIRECTORY:
             DSN----ACH.ACH470.FISRIF.DATA
             DSN----CPT.STMT.TRANS.FILE.DATA
             DSN----CPT.STMT.TRANS.FILE.INDEX
             DSN----SAV.ALT.NA.MASTER.FILE.DATA
             DSN----SAV.ALT.NA.MASTER.FILE.INDEX
             DSN----DDAT.TRANSFER.MASTER.DATA
             DSN----DDAT.TRANSFER.MASTER.INDEX

VOLUME -------- 335022
      HISTORY
          RELEASE----------------2
      CHARACTERISTICS
          BYTES/TRK--------------0          DEVTYPE---------........
          TRKS/CYL---------------0          VOLUME-TIMESTAMP:
          CYLS/VOL---------------0              X'9AE3CDA2AF9C3000'
      DATASPACE
          DATASETS---------------4          FORMAT-1-LABEL:
```

- VSAM.BATCH.ONE.UCAT

ATTRIBUTES:
SUBALLOC
EXPLICIT

SPACE-MAP----------FD1D4DFD120B

ATTRIBUTES--------(NULL)   EXTENTS----------------1
ATTRIBUTES--------(NULL)   EXTENTS----------------1
ATTRIBUTES--------(NULL)   EXTENTS----------------1

MAX-PHYREC-SZ----------0   DATASETS-ON-VOL-------70
MAX-EXT/ALLOC----------5   DATASPCS-ON-VOL--------1

ATTRIBUTES:
SUBALLOC
EXPLICIT

SPACE-MAP-----------OE10B43C3CFD016501FD3E3C

ATTRIBUTES--------(NULL)   EXTENTS----------------1
ATTRIBUTES--------(NULL)   EXTENTS----------------1
ATTRIBUTES--------(NULL)   EXTENTS----------------1
ATTRIBUTES--------(NULL)   EXTENTS----------------1
ATTRIBUTES--------(NULL)   EXTENTS----------------1
ATTRIBUTES--------(NULL)   EXTENTS----------------1
ATTRIBUTES--------(NULL)   EXTENTS----------------1

MAX-PHYREC-SZ----------0   DATASETS-ON-VOL-------71
MAX-EXT/ALLOC----------5   DATASPCS-ON-VOL--------1

ATTRIBUTES:

169

LISTING FROM CATALOG -

```
EXTENTS---------------1          CCHHR------X'0000001903'
SEC-ALLOC-------------0          TIMESTAMP
TYPE-----------CYLINDER              X'9AE3CDA2AF9C3000'
CLASS-----------------0
EXTENT-DESCRIPTOR:
TRACKS-TOTAL-------8310           BEG-CCHH-----X'00010000'
TRACKS-USED--------228
DATASET-DIRECTORY:
  DSN----CPT.STMT.MASTER.FILE.DATA
  DSN----CPT.STMT.MASTER.FILE.INDEX
  DSN----SAV.TRANSFER.MASTER.FILE.DATA
  DSN----SAV.TRANSFER.MASTER.FILE.INDEX
```

OUTPUT 9-13.

LISTING FROM CATALOG -- VSAM.BATCH.ONE.UCAT

```
THE NUMBER OF ENTRIES PROCESSED WAS:
          AIX  ------------------0
          CLUSTER  --------------0
          DATA  -----------------0
          INDEX  ----------------0
          NONVSAM  --------------0
          PATH  -----------------0
          SPACE  ----------------8
          USERCATALOG  ----------0
          TOTAL  ----------------8
```

THE NUMBER OF PROTECTED ENTRIES SUPPRESSED WAS 0

IDC0001I FUNCTION COMPLETED, HIGHEST CONDITION CODE WAS 0

170

- VSAM.BATCH.ONE.UCAT

SUBALLOC
EXPLICIT

SPACE-MAP----------C60C1EFD1F86

ATTRIBUTES--------(NULL)   EXTENTS----------------1
ATTRIBUTES--------(NULL)   EXTENTS----------------1
ATTRIBUTES--------(NULL)   EXTENTS----------------1
ATTRIBUTES--------(NULL)   EXTENTS----------------1

```
/ / JOB LISTCAT4
/ / EXEC IDCAMS,SIZE = AUTO
   LISTCAT -
      ALL
/*
/&
```

LISTCAT ALL output

```
CLUSTER ------- CICS.VS.TEMP.STORAGE
     HISTORY
          OWNER-IDENT------- (NULL)       CREATION----------86.307
          RELEASE----------------2        EXPIRATION--------00.000
     PROTECTION---------- (NULL)
     ASSOCIATIONS
          DATA-----CICS.VS.TEMP.STORAGE.DATA

DATA ------- CICS.VS.TEMP.STORAGE.DATA
     HISTORY
          OWNER-IDENT------- (NULL)       CREATION----------86.307
          RELEASE----------------2        EXPIRATION--------00.000
     PROTECTION---------- (NULL)
     ASSOCIATIONS
          CLUSTER--CICS.VS.TEMP.STORAGE
     ATTRIBUTES
          KEYLEN----------------0          AVGLRECL-----------2041
          RKP-------------------0          MAXLRECL-----------3780
          SHROPTNS(2,3)    RECOVERY        UNIQUE          NOERASE
          NOREPLICAT     UNORDERED         NOREUSE       NONSPANNED
     STATISTICS
          REC-TOTAL-------------0          SPLITS-CI-------------0
          REC-DELETED-----------0          SPLITS-CA-------------0
          REC-INSERTED----------0          FREESPACE-%CI---------0
          REC-UPDATED-----------0          FREESPACE-%CA---------0
          REC-RETRIEVED---------0          FREESPC-BYTES---------0
     ALLOCATION
          SPACE-TYPE------CYLINDER
          SPACE-PRI-------------20         USECLASS-PRI----------0
          SPACE-SEC-------------0          USECLASS-SEC----------0
     VOLUME
          VOLSER------------335009         PHYREC-SIZE--------4096
          DEVTYPE------X'3010200B'         PHYRECS/TRK-----------4
          VOLFLAG-----------PRIME          TRACKS/CA-----------30
          EXTENTS:
          LOW-CCHH-----X'010B0000'         LOW-RBA---------------0
          HIGH-CCHH----X'011E001D'         HIGH-RBA--------9830399

     VOLUME -------- DOSRES
          HISTORY
               RELEASE----------------2
          CHARACTERISTICS
               BYTES/TRK-------------0     DEVTYPE---------........
               TRKS/CYL-------------0      VOLUME-TIMESTAMP:
               CYLS/VOL-------------0          X'96F3AED95DE4A000'
          DATASPACE
               DATASETS-------------1      FORMAT-1-LABEL:
               EXTENTS--------------1      CCHHR------X'022A00000C'
               SEC-ALLOC-----------0       TIMESTAMP
```

OUTPUT 9-14.

BUFSPACE------------8192
EXCPEXIT----------(NULL)
NONINDEXED   VSAMDATSET

CISIZE--------------4096
CI/CA--------------120
NOWRITECHK   NOIMBED

EXCPS--------------2522
EXTENTS----------------1
SYSTEM-TIMESTAMP:
    X'9BC57365E5E04000'

HI-ALLOC-RBA-----9830400
HI-USED-RBA------9830400

HI-ALLOC-RBA-----9830400
HI-USED-RBA------9830400

EXTENT-NUMBER-----------1
EXTENT-TYPE--------X'00'

TRACKS---------------600

MAX-PHYREC-SZ----------0
MAX-EXT/ALLOC----------5

DATASETS-ON-VOL--------1
DATASPCS-ON-VOL--------1

ATTRIBUTES:
SUBALLOC
EXPLICIT

173

```
TYPE--------------TRACK                 X'96F3AED95DE4A000'
CLASS-------------------0
EXTENT-DESCRIPTOR:
TRACKS-TOTAL-----------30               BEG-CCHH-----X'00450000'
TRACKS-USED-----------30
DATASET-DIRECTORY:
   DSN----VSAM.MASTER.CATALOG

USERCATALOG --- VSAM.BATCH.ONE.UCAT
   HISTORY
      RELEASE----------------2
   VOLUMES
      VOLSER-----------335011           DEVTYPE------X'3010200B'

CLUSTER ------- VSAM.MASTER.CATALOG
   HISTORY
      OWNER-IDENT-------(NULL)          CREATION----------84.056
      RELEASE------------------2        EXPIRATION--------00.000
   PROTECTION----------(NULL)
   ASSOCIATIONS
      DATA-----VSAM.CATALOG.BASE.DATA.RECORD
      INDEX----VSAM.CATALOG.BASE.INDEX.RECORD

   DATA ------- VSAM.CATALOG.BASE.DATA.RECORD
   HISTORY
      OWNER-IDENT-------(NULL)          CREATION----------84.056
      RELEASE----------------2          EXPIRATION--------00.000
   PROTECTION----------(NULL)
   ASSOCIATIONS
      CLUSTER--VSAM.MASTER.CATALOG
   ATTRIBUTES
      KEYLEN----------------44          AVGLRECL------------505
      RKP-------------------0           MAXLRECL------------505
      SHROPTNS(3,3)   RECOVERY          SUBALLOC         NOERASE
      UNORDERED       NOREUSE           NONSPANNED
   STATISTICS
      REC-TOTAL------------17           SPLITS-CI------------0
      REC-DELETED----------0            SPLITS-CA------------0
      REC-INSERTED---------0            FREESPACE-%CI--------0
      REC-UPDATED----------0            FREESPACE-%CA--------0
      REC-RETRIEVED-----11358           FREESPC-BYTES----193536
   ALLOCATION
      SPACE-TYPE--------TRACK
      SPACE-PRI-----------27            USECLASS-PRI---------0
      SPACE-SEC------------3            USECLASS-SEC---------0
   VOLUME
      VOLSER-----------DOSRES           PHYREC-SIZE--------512
      DEVTYPE------X'3010200B'          PHYRECS/TRK---------27
      VOLFLAG-----------PRIME           TRACKS/CA-----------3
```

- VSAM.MASTER.CATALOG

MASTERCAT

SPACE-MAP----------1E

ATTRIBUTES-------(NULL)   EXTENTS----------------3

VOLFLAG------------PRIME

```
BUFSPACE------------3072       CISIZE---------------512
EXCPEXIT----------(NULL)       CI/CA----------------54
INDEXED           NOWRITECHK   IMBED           NOREPLICAT

EXCPS--------------3816
EXTENTS---------------2
SYSTEM-TIMESTAMP:
    X'9BC38AE5D15BE000'


HI-ALLOC-RBA------248832
HI-USED-RBA-------248832

HI-ALLOC-RBA------221184       EXTENT-NUMBER-----------1
HI-USED-RBA-------221184       EXTENT-TYPE--------X'00'
```

```
        LOW-KEY-------------00
        HIGH-KEY-----------3F
        HI-KEY-RBA--------219136
        EXTENTS:
        LOW-CCHH-----X'00450000'        LOW-RBA----------------0
        HIGH-CCHH----X'00450017'        HIGH-RBA----------221183
     VOLUME
        VOLSER-----------DOSRES         PHYREC-SIZE----------512
        DEVTYPE------X'3010200B'        PHYRECS/TRK-----------27
        VOLFLAG----------PRIME          TRACKS/CA-------------3
        LOW-KEY-------------40
        HIGH-KEY-----------FF
        HI-KEY-RBA--------221184
        EXTENTS:
        LOW-CCHH-----X'0045001B'        LOW-RBA----------221184
        HIGH-CCHH----X'0045001D'        HIGH-RBA----------248831

INDEX ------ VSAM.CATALOG.BASE.INDEX.RECORD
     HISTORY
        OWNER-IDENT-------(NULL)        CREATION---------84.056
        RELEASE--------------2          EXPIRATION--------00.000
     PROTECTION---------(NULL)
     ASSOCIATIONS
        CLUSTER--VSAM.MASTER.CATALOG
     ATTRIBUTES
        KEYLEN--------------44          AVGLRECL---------------0
        RKP-----------------0           MAXLRECL------------505
        SHROPTNS(3,3)    RECOVERY       SUBALLOC        NOERASE
        NOREUSE
     STATISTICS
        REC-TOTAL-----------3           SPLITS-CI--------------0
        REC-DELETED---------0           SPLITS-CA--------------0
        REC-INSERTED--------0           FREESPACE-%CI----------0
        REC-UPDATED---------0           FREESPACE-%CA----------0
        REC-RETRIEVED-------0           FREESPC-BYTES------44544
     ALLOCATION
        SPACE-TYPE--------TRACK
        SPACE-PRI-----------3           USECLASS-PRI-----------0
        SPACE-SEC-----------3           USECLASS-SEC-----------0
     VOLUME
        VOLSER-----------DOSRES         PHYREC-SIZE----------512
        DEVTYPE------X'3010200B'        PHYRECS/TRK-----------27
        VOLFLAG----------PRIME          TRACKS/CA-------------1
        EXTENTS:
        LOW-CCHH-----X'00450018'        LOW-RBA----------------0
        HIGH-CCHH----X'0045001A'        HIGH-RBA-----------41471
     VOLUME
        VOLSER-----------DOSRES         PHYREC-SIZE----------512
        DEVTYPE------X'3010200B'        PHYRECS/TRK-----------27
```

- VSAM.MASTER.CATALOG

TRACKS---------------24

HI-ALLOC-RBA------248832   EXTENT-NUMBER----------1
HI-USED-RBA-------248832   EXTENT-TYPE--------X'00'

TRACKS----------------3

BUFSPACE---------------0   CISIZE--------------512
EXCPEXIT----------(NULL)   CI/CA----------------27
NOWRITECHK   IMBED   NOREPLICAT   UNORDERED

EXCPS---------------413   INDEX:
EXTENTS--------------3   LEVELS----------------2
SYSTEM-TIMESTAMP: ENTRIES/SECT----------7
    X'9BC38AE5F45F0000'   SEQ-SET-RBA-------41472
                              HI-LEVEL-RBA----------0

HI-ALLOC-RBA-------46080
HI-USED-RBA--------46080

HI-ALLOC-RBA-------41472   EXTENT-NUMBER----------1
HI-USED-RBA----------512   EXTENT-TYPE--------X'00'

TRACKS----------------3

HI-ALLOC-RBA-------45568   EXTENT-NUMBER----------1
HI-USED-RBA--------45568   EXTENT-TYPE--------X'80'

177

```
                VOLFLAG-----------PRIME      TRACKS/CA--------------3
                LOW-KEY-------------00
                HIGH-KEY------------3F
                EXTENTS:
                LOW-CCHH-----X'0045000O'     LOW-RBA-----------41472
                HIGH-CCHH----X'00450017'     HIGH-RBA----------45567
                VOLUME
                VOLSER-----------DOSRES      PHYREC-SIZE---------512
                DEVTYPE------X'3010200B'     PHYRECS/TRK---------27
                VOLFLAG-----------PRIME      TRACKS/CA--------------3
                LOW-KEY-------------40
                HIGH-KEY------------FF
                EXTENTS:
                LOW-CCHH-----X'0045001B'     LOW-RBA-----------45568
                HIGH-CCHH----X'0045001D'     HIGH-RBA----------46079

USERCATALOG --- VSAM.ONL.TEST.UCAT
        HISTORY
                RELEASE----------------2
        VOLUMES
                VOLSER------------335029     DEVTYPE------X'3010200B'

USERCATALOG --- VSAM.ONLINE.UCAT
        HISTORY
                RELEASE----------------2
        VOLUMES
                VOLSER------------335010     DEVTYPE------X'3010200B'

VOLUME -------- 335009
        HISTORY
                RELEASE----------------2
        CHARACTERISTICS
                BYTES/TRK-------------0      DEVTYPE---------........
                TRKS/CYL--------------0      VOLUME-TIMESTAMP:
                CYLS/VOL--------------0          X'9BC571419EFC2000'
        DATASPACE
                DATASETS--------------1      FORMAT-1-LABEL:
                EXTENTS---------------1      CCHHR------X'022A00000C'
                SEC-ALLOC-------------0      TIMESTAMP
                TYPE-----------CYLINDER          X'9BC571419EFC2000'
                CLASS-----------------0
        EXTENT-DESCRIPTOR:
                TRACKS-TOTAL--------600      BEG-CCHH-----X'010B0000'
                TRACKS-USED---------600
        DATASET-DIRECTORY:
                DSN----CICS.VS.TEMP.STORAGE.DATA
```

OUTPUT 9-18.

LISTING FROM CATALOG -- VSAM.MASTER.CATALOG

THE NUMBER OF ENTRIES PROCESSED WAS:

```
AIX  ------------------0     NONVSAM ---------------0
CLUSTER ---------------2     PATH ------------------0
DATA ------------------2     SPACE -----------------2
INDEX -----------------1     USERCATALOG ----------3
                            TOTAL ---------------10
```

THE NUMBER OF PROTECTED ENTRIES SUPPRESSED WAS 0
IDC0001I FUNCTION COMPLETED, HIGHEST CONDITION CODE WAS 0

TRACKS---------------24

HI-ALLOC-RBA-------46080   EXTENT-NUMBER----------1
HI-USED-RBA--------46080   EXTENT-TYPE--------X'80'

TRACKS----------------3

VOLFLAG-----------PRIME

VOLFLAG-----------PRIME

MAX-PHYREC-SZ----------0   DATASETS-ON-VOL--------1
MAX-EXT/ALLOC----------5   DATASPCS-ON-VOL--------1

ATTRIBUTES:
UNIQUE
EXPLICIT

SPACE-MAP-----------FD0258

ATTRIBUTES--------(NULL)   EXTENTS----------------1

```
/ / JOB LISTCAT5
/ / EXEC IDCAMS,SIZE = AUTO
   LISTCAT -
      ALLOCATION
/*
/&
```

LISTCAT ALLOCATION output

```
CLUSTER ------- CICS.VS.TEMP.STORAGE
      HISTORY
         OWNER-IDENT-------(NULL)        CREATION----------86.307
         RELEASE----------------2         EXPIRATION--------00.000

      DATA ------- CICS.VS.TEMP.STORAGE.DATA
      HISTORY
         OWNER-IDENT-------(NULL)        CREATION----------86.307
         RELEASE----------------2         EXPIRATION--------00.000
      ALLOCATION
         SPACE-TYPE------CYLINDER
         SPACE-PRI------------20          USECLASS-PRI-----------0
         SPACE-SEC-------------0          USECLASS-SEC-----------0
      VOLUME
         VOLSER------------335009         PHYREC-SIZE---------4096
         DEVTYPE------X'30102030B'        PHYRECS/TRK-----------4
         VOLFLAG-----------PRIME          TRACKS/CA------------30
         EXTENTS:
         LOW-CCHH-----X'010B0000'         LOW-RBA----------------0
         HIGH-CCHH----X'011E001D'         HIGH-RBA--------9830399

CLUSTER ------- VSAM.MASTER.CATALOG
      HISTORY
         OWNER-IDENT-------(NULL)        CREATION----------84.056
         RELEASE----------------2         EXPIRATION--------00.000

      DATA ------- VSAM.CATALOG.BASE.DATA.RECORD
      HISTORY
         OWNER-IDENT-------(NULL)        CREATION----------84.056
         RELEASE----------------2         EXPIRATION--------00.000
      ALLOCATION
         SPACE-TYPE---------TRACK
         SPACE-PRI------------27          USECLASS-PRI-----------0
         SPACE-SEC-------------3          USECLASS-SEC-----------0
      VOLUME
         VOLSER-----------DOSRES          PHYREC-SIZE----------512
         DEVTYPE------X'30102008'         PHYRECS/TRK----------27
         VOLFLAG-----------PRIME          TRACKS/CA-------------3
         LOW-KEY--------------00
         HIGH-KEY-------------3F
         HI-KEY-RBA--------219136
         EXTENTS:
         LOW-CCHH-----X'00450000'         LOW-RBA----------------0
         HIGH-CCHH----X'00450017'         HIGH-RBA---------221183
      VOLUME
         VOLSER-----------DOSRES          PHYREC-SIZE----------512
         DEVTYPE------X'30102008'         PHYRECS/TRK----------27
         VOLFLAG-----------PRIME          TRACKS/CA-------------3
```

```
HI-ALLOC-RBA-----9830400
HI-USED-RBA------9830400

HI-ALLOC-RBA-----9830400        EXTENT-NUMBER----------1
HI-USED-RBA------9830400        EXTENT-TYPE-------X'00'

TRACKS---------------600
```

```
HI-ALLOC-RBA------248832
HI-USED-RBA-------248832

HI-ALLOC-RBA------221184        EXTENT-NUMBER----------1
HI-USED-RBA-------221184        EXTENT-TYPE-------X'00'

TRACKS---------------24

HI-ALLOC-RBA------248832        EXTENT-NUMBER----------1
HI-USED-RBA-------248832        EXTENT-TYPE-------X'00'
```

```
            LOW-KEY---------------40
            HIGH-KEY-------------FF
            HI-KEY-RBA--------221184
            EXTENTS:
            LOW-CCHH-----X'0045001B'        LOW-RBA----------221184
            HIGH-CCHH----X'0045001D'        HIGH-RBA---------248831

    INDEX ------ VSAM.CATALOG.BASE.INDEX.RECORD
        HISTORY
            OWNER-IDENT-------(NULL)         CREATION----------84.056
            RELEASE----------------2         EXPIRATION--------00.000
        ALLOCATION
            SPACE-TYPE---------TRACK
            SPACE-PRI--------------3         USECLASS-PRI-----------0
            SPACE-SEC--------------3         USECLASS-SEC-----------0
        VOLUME
            VOLSER------------DOSRES         PHYREC-SIZE----------512
            DEVTYPE------X'3010200B'         PHYRECS/TRK-----------27
            VOLFLAG------------PRIME         TRACKS/CA-------------1
            EXTENTS:
            LOW-CCHH-----X'00450018'         LOW-RBA----------------0
            HIGH-CCHH----X'0045001A'         HIGH-RBA-----------41471
        VOLUME
            VOLSER------------DOSRES         PHYREC-SIZE----------512
            DEVTYPE------X'3010200B'         PHYRECS/TRK-----------27
            VOLFLAG------------PRIME         TRACKS/CA-------------3
            LOW-KEY---------------00
            HIGH-KEY-------------3F
            EXTENTS:
            LOW-CCHH-----X'00450000'         LOW-RBA------------41472
            HIGH-CCHH----X'00450017'         HIGH-RBA-----------45567
        VOLUME
            VOLSER------------DOSRES         PHYREC-SIZE----------512
            DEVTYPE------X'3010200B'         PHYRECS/TRK-----------27
            VOLFLAG------------PRIME         TRACKS/CA-------------3
            LOW-KEY---------------40
            HIGH-KEY-------------FF
            EXTENTS:
            LOW-CCHH-----X'0045001B'         LOW-RBA------------45568
            HIGH-CCHH----X'0045001D'         HIGH-RBA-----------46079
```

- VSAM.MASTER.CATALOG

TRACKS------------------3

HI-ALLOC-RBA--------46080
HI-USED-RBA---------46080

HI-ALLOC-RBA-------41472   EXTENT-NUMBER-----------1
HI-USED-RBA-----------512   EXTENT-TYPE---------X'00'

TRACKS------------------3

HI-ALLOC-RBA-------45568   EXTENT-NUMBER-----------1
HI-USED-RBA--------45568   EXTENT-TYPE---------X'80'

TRACKS------------------24

HI-ALLOC-RBA-------46080   EXTENT-NUMBER-----------1
HI-USED-RBA--------46080   EXTENT-TYPE---------X'80'

TRACKS------------------3

```
LISTING FROM CATALOG -- VSAM.MASTER.CATALOG

THE NUMBER OF ENTRIES PROCESSED WAS:
                    AIX --------------------0
                    CLUSTER ----------------2
                    DATA -------------------2
                    INDEX ------------------1
                    NONVSAM ----------------0
                    PATH -------------------0
                    SPACE ------------------0
                    USERCATALOG ------------0
                    TOTAL ------------------5

    THE NUMBER OF PROTECTED ENTRIES SUPPRESSED WAS 0

IDC0001I FUNCTION COMPLETED, HIGHEST CONDITION CODE WAS 0
```

The remainder of this chapter offers some advice on how to better utilize DASD and processing time when it comes to VSAM. A sample worksheet has been included. Add your own considerations to it. Work with it. Tailor the form to meet your demands. But the point remains—monitor those VSAM files!

What should you be looking for when reviewing the output from a LISTCAT? Examples of potential problem areas are:

1. Suballocation—If the object has experienced suballocation, it might be time to perform a backup operation on the object with a subsequent restore.
2. CI/CA splits—A warning sign of a need for reorganization. VSAM might be creating too much freespace.
3. Hi-Used-RBA—Reveals that the cluster might be approaching the end of allocated space.

AMS PERFORMANCE-RELATED PARAMETERS

When you're working with AMS, most commands need only a few parameters in order to successfully execute. In other words, most parameters are optional. Default values will nearly always be assumed. Several parameters associated with the DEFINE CLUSTER command in particular influence performance. These parameters are:

CONTROLINTERVALSIZE
FREESPACE

REPLICATE
IMBED
BUFFERSPACE
KEYRANGES
ORDERED
SPEED | RECOVERY
WRITECHECK

Is it always wise to let VSAM assume default values? No. Depending on the option and your processing environment, default values can reduce efficiency. DASD space as well as run time can be wasted. Let's take a look at some specific areas all VSAM coders need to be aware of:

Control Interval Size

The CONTROLINTERVALSIZE parameter can be coded at the cluster or the components level. You can also let VSAM calculate CISIZE automatically. So what's the best choice? A good rule of thumb is to code the CISIZE associated with the data component, but to let VSAM choose the CISIZE for the index component.

When selecting a CISIZE for the data component, consider how the file will be processed. Generally, a small CISIZE (4096 bytes or less) is best when the file is used mostly for random retrieval. Sequential processing fares better if a large CISIZE (greater than 4096 bytes) is used.

DASD model is another important consideration. CIs are actually stored on DASD in physical records. The physical records might be smaller than CISIZE because of hardware configurations. Only four sizes of physical records exist for VSAM: 512, 1024, 2048 and 4096. When writing CIs to DASD, VSAM selects the largest physical record size that divides evenly into the selected CISIZE. Usually the larger the physical record, the better the space is used on each track. A CISIZE that's a multiple of 4096 is generally the best choice.

Freespace

Freespace is a major performance factor. It exists on two levels:

1. The percentage of freespace in a CI.
2. The percentage of free CIs in a CA.

An optimum amount of freespace reduces the likelihood of CI and CA splits. Both are expensive when it comes to processing time because splits increase the chance of moving records to a different cylinder. Such movement shifts records farther from others in key sequence.

When allocating freespace, consider the following factors:
1. Estimated growth of the file.
2. CI size.
3. Size of data records to be added or lengthened.
4. Distribution of changes throughout the file.

Unless your file always remains constant, freespace allocation changes. Add a record and freespace decreases. Delete a record from a KSDS, and it increases. If you keep adding records but fail to adjust freespace, CI and CA splits will occur and eventually allocated file space will be exceeded.

Freespace allocations are determined by the DEFINE CLUSTER command. Freespace is allocated in terms of bytes, not records. The parameter uses percentages when allocating. For example, you can tell VSAM to reserve 20 percent of the space in a 4096-byte CI as freespace. This actually means that 819 bytes are left empty in each CI. Now depending on your logical record size, this may or may not be a wise allocation. If a data record consists of 800 bytes, each CI has only room enough for one.

To obtain more freespace, reload the file with the REPRO command. If the freespace is being used up frequently, look at raising the percentage. But a bit of advice; don't overly allocate freespace. You'll only succeed in wasting DASD space, and sequential processing will be degraded. Run a LISTCAT periodically and monitor the freespace—that's the best way to maintain it at a proper level.

Replicate/Imbed

When defining a KSDS cluster, you can use the IMBED and REPLICATE parameters. Both of these parameters change the way the KSDS's index component is stored. You can code these parameters at either the CLUSTER or INDEX level; the results are the same.

REPLICATE says that all records of the index set will be replicated on a track of the index. One index record will be duplicated as many times as it fits on a track. The advantage of this option is that it reduces time lost in waiting for the index record to rotate around to be read. The disadvantage is that a full track is required for each replicated index record.

In simple terms, whether or not to replicate is a matter of DASD space vs. processing speed. Most of the time, REPLICATE offers the greatest effect when insufficient buffer space is available for the index, and records are being retrieved via direct access. Why does bufferspace influence the choice? Because buffer space too has a major impact on performance.

REPLICATE and IMBED are two options that tend to go hand in hand. IMBED moves sequence set records from the space allocated to the index set and places them in the space allocated to the data component. To really understand why IMBED offers advantages, you need to understand what goes on physically with a VSAM file. The first track of each CA is where the sequence set record that corresponds to that CA is stored. This means that a sequence set record and all the CIs it indexes can be accessed with one seek. Since a seek requires movement of the DASD's access mechanism, the fewer seeks you have, the quicker access is accomplished.

Back to the relationship between REPLICATE and IMBED. Because REPLICATE duplicates the index set records, the sequence set records are automatically duplicated. Add in the IMBED parameter, and these duplicated sequence set records are stored with the data component's CA. You've achieved less rotational delay and fewer seeks.

It is not necessary to use the REPLICATE and IMBED options as a team. Sometimes they do make a good team effort, but they can be used independent of one another. Many data centers choose to use good buffering techniques and the IMBED option only. Improved buffer allocation often eliminates the need for REPLICATE and thus saves DASD space.

Why not always rely on buffers rather than the IMBED option? Sometimes you're not in full control of buffer sizes. Neither CICS nor IMS jobs allow you full control over this feature.

IMBED, like most options, naturally has some disadvantages. It increases the space requirements of the file's data component. Also, performance will only be improved if the file's index buffer size is correctly allocated. You must provide enough buffer space for the entire index set to reside in virtual storage.

Buffer Space

Buffer size is probably the most important performance factor. Buffers are used for I/O operations. The better they are, the quicker I/O operations will occur.

Basically VSAM transfers the contents of a CI to an I/O buffer in virtual storage. Because of this transfer, buffers must have sufficient space to handle whatever size the CI happens to be. In other words, there's a direct relationship between CI size and buffer size.

You can use the BUFFERSPACE parameter to control both data and index buffers. A data buffer contains the data CI holding the record being referenced. An index buffer contains the sequence set or index set record needed to locate the data record.

Better sequential processing usually can be achieved when buffer size is large enough to hold four to five data buffers. Direct processing benefits from good buffer allocations when multiple index buffers can exist.

You can specify buffer size in the DEFINE command or through a DLBL statement. If you want to use the DLBL parameter, however, the size specified must be larger than the catalog entry's buffer allocation. VSAM automatically rounds whatever you allocate for buffer size to the nearest CI size boundary. For example, if 13000 was specified, VSAM would round it to 13284.

Buffer space, like most cluster features, can be allowed to default. A word of warning though: VSAM will default to the smallest amount of buffer space possible, and that is not always the best choice. Unless you tell it otherwise, VSAM allocates two data buffers and one index buffer.

There's another little trick it's nice to be aware of. Buffer space can be set by the BUFFERSPACE parameter for the DEFINE CLUSTER command. This is the value all related application jobs will use unless another value is coded through a job's DLBL statement. In other words, the latter can override whatever is specified at the cluster level when it comes to buffer size. Be aware, however, that if you specify a smaller amount on the DLBL statement than that contained in the DEFINE command, VSAM takes the amount in the DEFINE command.

Basically the steps to follow when making buffer allocations are:

1. Determine how many data and index buffers to use.
2. Determine how many bytes of storage are required to accommodate the necessary number of buffers.

The way the file is accessed influences buffer space. Sequential processing requires one index buffer with the remaining space given to data buffers. On the other hand, random processing requires two data buffers with the remaining space given to index buffers. Now let's take a more in-depth look at how to improve performance.

Sequential processing improvements can be achieved by increasing the number of data buffers. However, index buffer allocations have no impact; the default size performs just as well as any other allocation because sequential processing doesn't rely on index keys. Of course when dealing with an ESDS or an RRDS, it's not even necessary to allocate an index buffer, since neither supports indexing.

An increased number of data buffers helps VSAM overlap I/O operations and the processing of data. VSAM uses half of the data buffers for I/O operations and half for processing. Another benefit reaped from good data buffer allocations is that with each I/O operation VSAM reads or writes as many CIs as possible. The more buffers allocated, the few I/O operations are required to process a file. I recommend, though, that you do not allocate so much buffer space that an I/O operation references an entire CA. That's just too much! The best approach is to allocate enough buffer space for VSAM to reference two tracks of data at a time. By the way, the reason we say "two" is in order to allow for overlap.

For a cluster being processed sequentially, find out how many CIs are in each track. Double that number for the sake of overlap. Then add one for an extra buffer. VSAM needs the latter in order to handle such internal processing conditions as CI splits. Multiply the resulting number by the data component's CI size in order to provide for the index buffer.

Random processing requires only two data buffers. Performance benefits are realized by allocating additional index buffers. The best performance will be realized if enough index buffers are available to hold in virtual storage the entire index set plus one sequence set record. If all of this can be stored at the same time and the IMBED parameter is also specified, no extra movements are needed by the DASD's access mechanism to process index records.

For a cluster being processed randomly, find out how many records are in the index set by running a LISTCAT. It shows how many records are in an index component. Be aware, though, that this number represents both sequence set and index set records. To get the number you need for allocation purposes, subtract from this number the number of sequence set records contained in the data set. There's one sequence set record for each cylinder used, so determine how many cylinders are in use and you'll have the number of sequence set records.

Three pieces of information exhibited by a LISTCAT allow you to make this computation:

1. CISIZE
2. CI/CA
3. HI-USED-RBA

Multiply CISIZE by CI/CA in order to get the number of bytes per CA. Divide this number into HI-USED-RBA and round up.

The result is the number of CAs in use, which is the same as the number of sequence set records.

Keyrangers/Ordered

The KEYRANGES parameter applies only to a KSDS. This VSAM feature allows you to place specific ranges of keys on different volumes. For example, in our Inventory System items with number 1 through 500 could be placed on one volume; item numbers 501 through 1000 on another volume; etc.

In effect you've distributed the cluster's data component across several DASD volumes. This is a really good performance booster if the file is heavily used because it eliminates so much contention for just one volume.

No discussion about KEYRANGES would be complete without mentioning the ORDERED parameter. This parameter instructs VSAM to use allocated DASD volumes in the order in which they're listed. Normally one range of keys is placed on each volume; therefore, the number of key ranges you have is the number of volumes you need. What if the numbers aren't equal? If key ranges exceed volumes, then usage will simply start over with the first volume listed. If volumes exceed key ranges, it doesn't matter since that particular cluster just won't use them.

Speed/Recovery

When you are defining a cluster, one of the decisions to make is SPEED vs. RECOVERY. The default value is RECOVERY. These parameters influence how data is loaded to a file and what steps must occur if such a load fails.

RECOVERY results in a preformatting of each allocated CA with binary zeros before any CIs are written to the CA. Realize that this preformatting does take extra time. SPEED, on the other hand, involves no preformatting; thus it's quicker to load a file under this option.

If SPEED is the quickest and good performance is the name of the game, why even consider RECOVERY?

As its name implies, RECOVERY assists in recovering a load operation if it fails. Because of the preformatting, the load can be started over at the point of failure instead of the very beginning. If it's a large file, RECOVERY can be a great time saver when a load fails. However, because of the internal workings of VSAM, RECOVERY is limited to an ESDS. It can be coded for a KSDS or RRDS, but in actual practice it does nothing for you.

Most of the time, SPEED is the best choice. The only exception is when a large ESDS is being loaded to DASD and there is not ample time to restart it from the very beginning.

Writecheck

WRITECHECK says that each time a data record is written, it must be followed by a subsequent READ operation. The latter isn't something you have to include in an application program. VSAM takes care of it automatically if the WRITECHECK option is specified.

By reading a record after it's written, VSAM can check to see whether it was successfully written. It's a good way to check data integrity. The negative side of this feature, though, is that more processing time is involved. In effect, each record that is written is actually accessed twice.

If time is important and you feel fairly secure with data integrity, I recommend that you not use this option. If omitted, the default value is NOWRITECHECK.

OTHER PERFORMANCE FACTORS

Cluster options aren't the only factors that can influence performance. Data set placement is another consideration. Some good tips are:

1. Allocate multiple data spaces on a DASD volume. Critical files should be placed in preferred data space.
2. Define critical files before noncritical files within a data space.
3. Be consistent in CA size for data and index components. If one is a cylinder, make the other a cylinder also.
4. Make space allocations at the cluster level, rather than at the components levels.

5. Look at spreading a VSAM file across volumes. Contention by the access mechanism will be reduced.

6. Consider placing the index component of a KSDS on a DASD type different from that housing the data component. A faster DASD type for the index component can speed up indexing and thus record retrieval time.

Following is a sample worksheet for monitoring a cluster's performance. Run LISTCAT first and then try our worksheet to help you make some tuning efficiencies.

General Reminders

The defines for your VSAM files should be disbursed evenly amoung the different volumes. This method allows for a more efficient use of the VSAM space, and will allow defines to run more quickly. For example:

```
Inefficient VSAM define:
Define Cluster -
  ( NAME(VSAM.FILE1) -
  VOLUME(335005 335011 335012 335021 335022) ) -
  . . .
Define cluster -
  ( NAME(VSAM.FILE2) -
  VOLUME(335005 335011 335012 335021 335022) ) -
  . . .
Correct VSAM define:
Define cluster -
  ( NAME(VSAM.FILE1) -
  VOLUME(335022 335021 335005 335011 335012) ) -
  . . .
```

A high number of excps (greater than 80,000) is an indication of trouble with the VSAM file. If this occurs, the defines for the file should be reexamined carefully and modified.

Remember when you are examining a listcat that the information should be taken from the data component of the file and not from the index component.

DOS VSAM for Application Programmers

VSAM MONITORING WORKSHEET

NAME OF FILE: _____

PGMR: _____ DATE: _____

It is suggested that these worksheets be retained for 3 month periods in order to more carefully monitor the use of VSAM space.

Please Note:

Steps 1 through 11 are calculations that can be used if your file has 0 percent CI and CA-FREESPACE, or a certain percentage of CI-FREESPACE but 0 percent CA-FREESPACE. It is virtually impossible to obtain an accurate calculation for a file with CA-FREESPACE. This is why it is very important to monitor these files regularly in order to correct a problem with suballocation before it becomes critical.

1. Looking at the index area for the file, if the extents for this file are greater than 1. The primary and possibly the secondary allocations for the file need to be recalculated. If the file has only one extent, you might want to recalculate the number of cylinders needed to avoid overallocation.

2. What is the AVGLRECL for the file?_____

3. What is the FREESPACE-%CI for the file?_____

4. Multiply FREESPACE-%CI by .001 for the file?____

5. What is the PHYREC-SIZE of the file?_____

6. If value from step 3 is zero, simply place the value from step 5 in the final blank for this calculation and go to step 7. Multiply value from step 4 by value from step 5. (If fraction, round up) Subtract this value from the PHYREC-SIZE for the file (step 5)._____ (This value is the new PHYREC-SIZE for the file, which takes into consideration distributed freespace.)

194

7. Divide AVERCL into new PHYREC-SIZE (final value from step 6 calculations)_____ (If this value is a fraction, use only the whole number, unrounded.)

8. Multiply the value from step 7 by PHYRECS/TRK._____ (This value is the number of logical records per track.)

9. Multiply the number of logical records per track (value from step 8) by the TRACKS/CA._____ (This value is the number of logical records that will fit on one cylinder.)

10. What is the REC-TOTAL for the file?_____

11. Divide the value from step 9 into the REC-TOTAL (step 10) for the file._____ (If this is a fraction, round up to whole number. This is the number of primary cylinders needed to keep the file from using more than one extent. If after the above calculation, the number of cylinders needed is considerably different than the current allocation, this allocation should be adjusted.)

The secondary allocations for the file will be allocated up to 18 times. After this point, the file runs out of room, and problems arise. The file should never reach this point with careful monitoring, however.

12. How many CA-SPLITS does the file have?_____ If this value is greater than 0, the %CA-FREESPACE for the file should be increased.

13. How many CI-SPLITS does the file have?_____ If this value is greater than 0, the %CI-FREESPACE for the file should be increased.

CI-SPLITS are not as important to monitor as CA-SPLITS. If there are any CA-SPLITS, you will probably have a large number of CI-SPLITS.

14. Have any records been inserted?_____ Last month?_____ If file is not random access and therefore no records are being inserted, there is no need for freespace.

15. What is this month's HI-ALLOC-RBA?_____

16. What is this month's HI-USED-RBA?_____

Last month's?_____

These allocated and used RBAs should be the same. The file should be monitored for a couple of months in order to get an accurate value of what is being used.

17. There are no set rules for calculating the BUFFERSPACE and CISIZE to use with a file. This is a very gray area and is left to you. Some things are not acceptable, however, and you should consult the above-mentioned manuals for more information on these areas.

It would be impossible to include all of the information on this checklist without it turning into another manual. A few of the more important items are outlined below, however. These are not to be taken as rules for calculating parameters, and are only to serve as reminders to you.

A.   Do not specify BUFFERSPACE at both the cluster and data component levels. Consult *VSE/VSAM PROGRAMMER'S REFERENCE* for more details.

B.   If buffer space is omitted, a default value will be set in the catalog. This will be the minimum amount of buffer space allowed by VSAM.

C.   It is usually not a good idea to specify CISIZE at the cluster level because size will then apply both to the data and index portions of the file.

D.   If CISIZE is not specified, VSAM will determine it for you.

E.   CISIZE for on-line files should be as small as possible, and BUFFERSPACE should be left to VSAM to calculate. CISIZE for batch files should be as large as possible, and BUFFERSPACE should be calculated for these files to use excess virtual storage. The BUFFERSPACE parameter can be included in the VSAM catalog, or placed on the DLBL for the file in your JCL.

10
CHAPTER

Recovery
and Security
Considerations

Regardless of the access method used, recovery and security considerations should always be part of your methodology. Data is the most valuable resource managed by any data center. Without data, why would we even be in business?

VSAM offers more recovery and security considerations than other access methods. Special facilities exist that help users achieve improved data integrity. For example, a file can be protected against unauthorized usage through passwords. Different levels of passwords are available to grant the authority to read or update a file, to update a catalog, etc.

Accurate and easy recovery measures can save a data center from disaster. Imagine what it would be like if all of your DASD volumes were suddenly destroyed and there were no backup tapes to restore for master files? A few simple steps each day can save any data center from such a bleak picture. VSAM provides easy-to-use commands for copying and restoring clusters and catalogs.

In a VSAM environment, catalog recovery is especially important. Since the catalog plays such a major role, I strongly recommend establishing user catalogs. A master catalog alone attaches too much responsibility to one catalog.

In the next few pages, I will show you some of the AMS commands for a backup/recovery plan. When designing such a plan, it's important to remember that the VSAM file is attached to a catalog. That's why it's so important to include in your plan provisions for backing-up related catalog information whenever a file is copied.

Designing a good backup/recovery plan isn't a quick and simple task. It takes a great deal of thought to properly ensure that processing can continue in spite of a disaster. Data centers differ in such plans because their needs are different. More often than not, several key people are involved in developing the plan; both programming and operations personnel need to actively participate in this type of effort. A backup/recovery plan is something that needs to be reviewed periodically because operating schedules and demands change. Also, don't forget to test it. Just because things look good on paper doesn't mean they work!

Now, let's look at some of the AMS commands you'll need for a backup/recovery plan.

EXPORT/IMPORT—A TEAM EFFORT

The EXPORT and IMPORT commands work in conjunction with one another. These commands allow you to:

1) Move objects from one operating system to another, such as a DOS to MVS conversion.

2) Take backup copies of objects.

3) Restore backup copies of objects and update related catalog entries.

4) Sever relationships between user catalogs and the master catalog.

Note that I used the term "objects" several times. An object in the case of the EXPORT/IMPORT command can mean a cluster, alternate index, or user catalog. Paths are not exportable by themselves; however, they are automatically included when an alternate index or cluster is moved.

EXPORT produces a backup copy. IMPORT restores the exported backup. If you have difficulty remembering which command does what, think of it like this. The EXPORT command copies a file so that it can be taken elsewhere and used; it can *export* the object outside of its native environment just like we export products to foreign countries. IMPORT *brings* an object into the local environment just as imported goods are shipped into our country. By the way, once a file is copied with EXPORT, it remains the same on DASD until it's deleted.

Objects can be exported to other DASD volumes or to tape. Generally, a backup/recovery plan calls for tape copies which should be stored in secured areas. If possible, make additional copies of the really important files and place them off-site in case your building is physically damaged.

Another facility provided by the EXPORT command is a means to disconnect user catalogs from a master catalog. Why would you want to do this? Perhaps there is no longer a need for a specific user catalog. It may be desirable to move a certain user catalog to another system. In any event, whenever the disconnect feature of the EXPORT command is used, the user catalog itself is not actually copied; it remains intact on its original volume. All the disconnect does is to sever the relationship. If you need a copy of the catalog, use the EXPORT command to copy it prior to running the disconnect.

You might say that the IMPORT command works in reverse of the EXPORT command. It restores objects which have been copied by the EXPORT command and connects user catalogs to the master catalog.

There are other ways to copy objects besides EXPORT/IMPORT. You can write programs to perform the same functions. The REPRO command is still another alternative.

REPRO is a very popular method for copying and restoring files. Unlike EXPORT/IMPORT, the REPRO command copies a file in a special format that includes all information needed to automatically define it. In other words, if REPRO is used to restore a file, a DEFINE command must precede it. On the other hand, a DEFINE command will not be needed when IMPORT is used.

On the surface, it probably seems like EXPORT/IMPORT commands are better than REPRO. In reality, that may not be true, depending on the time that is available. Both EXPORT and IMPORT require the most processing time. It's often quicker to run a DEFINE followed by a REPRO rather than the "all-in-one" IMPORT command.

JCL REQUIREMENTS

EXPORT/IMPORT require special JCL provisions.

Export

1) Assignment for user catalog housing the exported object.

2) A DLBL statement for the object being exported.

3) A DLBL or TLBL statement for the file created as a result of the EXPORT operation.

4) For a tape device, you must use SYS005 in the ASSGN statement.

Import

1) Assignment for user catalog housing the imported object.

2) A DLBL or TLBL statement for the file created as a result of the EXPORT operation.

3) A DLBL statement for the VSAM file to be restored.

4) For a tape device, you must use SYS004 in the ASSGN statement.

EXPORT

The EXPORT command has two different formats. First, let's look at the format used to disconnect a user catalog from the master catalog:

EXPORT entryname [/password] DISCONNECT

Here, the value coded for *entryname* is the name of the user catalog to be disconnected. If applicable, the catalog's *password* must also be included.

To move or copy a file, use the following format:

EXPORT entryname [/password]
    INFILE(filename)

OUTFILE(filename ENVIRONMENT (subparameters))
[TEMPORARY | PERMANENT]

The following are required parameters:

entryname The value coded for *entryname* is the name of the object to be exported. If applicable, the object's *password* must also be included.

INFILE May be abbreviated as IFILE. *filename* specifies the same used on the DLBL statement for the object being exported.

OUTFILE May be abbreviated as OFILE. *filename* specifies the same used on the DLBL or TLBL statement for the file to be created by the EXPORT operation.

ENVIRONMENT May be abbreviated as ENV. The sub-parameters following the ENVIRONMENT parameter describe the output file's characteristics.

  BLOCKSIZE
  May be abbreviated as BLKSZ. Specifies in bytes the block size of the output copy. The default value is 2048.

  NOLABEL|STDLABEL
  May be abbreviated as NLBL and SLBL respectively. Applicable only if the exported copy is written to tape. Specifies the type of tape label to be written. NOLABEL says that the label will be omitted, and STDLABEL says that standard labels will be written. The default value is STDLABEL.

  PRIMEDATADEVICE (devtype)
  May be abbreviated as PDEV. Specifies the device type of the volume that contains the exported copy. 2400 identifies all tape devices. The default value is 2314.

TEMPORARY|PERMANENT May be abbreviated as TEMP and PERM respectively. Specifies whether the cluster being exported is to be deleted from the catalog once the EXPORT operation is complete. TEMPORARY "says" that the cluster is not to be deleted. PERMANENT "says" that the cluster is to be deleted. The default value is PERMANENT.

The following EXPORT job writes a VSAM cluster to tape. Since the TEMPORARY parameter is used, the cluster is not deleted from the user catalog.

```
/ /  JOB EXPORT
/ /  ASSGN SYS001,DISK,VOL = UCAT01,SHR
/ /  DLBL IJSYSUC,'USER.CATALOG', ,VSAM
/ /  EXTENT SYS001,UCAT01
/ /  DLBL SOURCE, 'KSDS.FILE', ,VSAM
/ /  EXTENT SYS001,UCAT01
/ /  ASSGN SYS005,TAPE
/ /  TLBL RECEIVE,'BACKUP.TAPE'
/ /  EXEC IDCAMS,SIZE = AUTO
     EXPORT -
        KSDS.FILE -
        INFILE(SOURCE) -
        OUTFILE(RECEIVE -
           ENV(PDEV(2400)   STDLABEL)) -
        TEMPORARY
/*
/&
```

Note the inclusion of DLBL IJSYSUC. Label information for the user catalog is required unless a job catalog is present. Otherwise, VSAM will try to reference the master catalog.

The following is an example of using EXPORT to disconnect a user catalog:

```
/ /  JOB DISCONN
//   EXEC IDCAMS,SIZE = AUTO
     EXPORT USER.CATALOG.ONE   DISCONNECT
/*
/&
```

When the DISCONNECT facility is used, no ASSGNs are needed.

IMPORT

The IMPORT command has two different formats. First, let's look at the format used to connect a user catalog to the master catalog.

OBJECTS(entryname DEVICE(devtype) VOLUMES(volser))
[CATALOG(catname[/password])]

entryname	The value coded for *entryname* is the name of the user catalog.
DEVICE	May be abbreviated as DEVT. *devtype* specifies the device type of the DASD volume containing the user catalog.
VOLUMES	May be abbreviated as VOL. *volser* specifies the DASD volume on which the user catalog resides.
CATALOG	May be abbreviated as CAT. *catname* specifies the name of the master catalog. The CAT parameter is required only if the master catalog is password protected.

To restore a file, use the following format:

IMPORT INFILE(filename ENVIRONMENT(subparameters))
    OUTFILE(filename)
    [PURGE | NOPURGE]
    CATALOG(catname[/password])]

The following are required parameters:

INFILE	May be abbreviated as IFILE. *filename* specifies the same used on the DLBL or TLBL statement for the object to be imported.
OUTFILE	May be abbreviated as OFILE. *filename* specifies the same used on the DLBL statement for the file to be created by the IMPORT operation.

The following are optional parameters:

ENVIRONMENT May be abbreviated as ENV. The subparameters following the ENVIRONMENT parameter describe the input file's characteristics.

BLOCKSIZE
May be abbreviated as BLKSZ. Specifies in bytes the block size of the copy created by the related EXPORT operation. The default value is 2048.

NOLABEL | STDLABEL
May be abbreviated as NLBL and SLBL respectively. Applicable only if the imported object is written to tape. Specifies the type of tape label written by the related EXPORT operation. NOLABEL says that the label will be omitted, and STDLABEL says that standard labels will be written. The default value is STDLABEL.

PRIMEDATADEVICE (devtype)
May be abbreviated as PDEV. Specifies the device type of the volume that contains the input object. 2400 identifies all tape devices. The default value is 2314.

PURGE | NOPURGE   May be abbreviated as PRG and NPRG respectively. PURGE allows the IMPORT operation to continue whether or not an existing file with the same name has expired. If a file with the same name already exists, NOPURGE will allow the IMPORT operation to proceed only if the existing file's expiration data has ocurred. The default value is NOPURGE.

CATALOG   May be abbreviated as CAT. *catname* specifies the name of the catalog which is to house the imported file. If the user catalog is password protected, the CATALOG parameter is required. This parameter is also required when you want to enter the imported file in the master catalog.

The following IMPORT job loads a VSAM cluster from tape to DASD:

```
/ / JOB IMPORT
/ / ASSGN SYS001,DISK,VOL = UCAT01,SHR
/ / DLBL IJSYSUC,'USER.CATALOG',,VSAM
/ / EXTENT SYS001,UCAT01
/ / ASSGN SYS004,TAPE
```

```
/ / TLBL SOURCE,'BACKUP.TAPE'
/ / DLBL RECEIVE,'KSDS.FILE',,VSAM
/ / EXTENT SYS001,UCAT01
/ / EXEC IDCAMS,SIZE = AUTO
   IMPORT -
       INFILE(SOURCE -
         ENV(PDEV(2400)   STDLABEL)) -
       OUTFILE(RECEIVE) -
       CATALOG(USER.CATALOG/USERMPW)
/*
/&
```

Note the DLBL IJSYSUC. Label information for the user catalog is required unless a job catalog is present. Otherwise, VSAM will try to reference the master catalog. Also, since the user catalog is password protected, the inclusion of the CATALOG parameter is necessary.

The following is an example of using IMPORT to connect a user catalog to the master catalog:

```
/ / JOB CONN
/ / EXEC IDCAMS,SIZE = AUTO
   IMPORT CONNECT -
       OBJECTS
         (USER.CATALOG.ONE -
         DEVICE(3340) -
         VOLUMES(UCAT01)
/*
/&
```

When the CONNECT facility is used, no ASSGNs are needed.

CATALOG RECOVERY

Although EXPORT/IMPORT can be used to transport catalogs from one system to another, catalog recovery is an entirely different subject. If appropriate backup procedures are in place, it's easy to recover files. All you have to do is run an IMPORT to restore the most current file and then restart processing.

Catalogs can and do become damaged from time to time. For example, the DASD volume housing a catalog can experience physical problems. Sometimes a catalog will be so badly damaged that recovery is impossible.

AMS provides special commands to assist in catalog recovery. Since in most data centers the programming staff has this responsibility, I've elected to simply introduce these commands rather than explore them in detail.

Whether or not these commands can be used depends on one condition—the catalog in question must have been defined as *recoverable.* When coding a DEFINE USERCATALOG, one of the optional parameters is RECOVERABLE. Unless specified otherwise, the catalog will not be recoverable. Guidelines as to whether catalogs are recoverable is an important part of the disaster recovery plan every data center should develop.

What do we mean by a "recoverable catalog"?

Obviously, it sounds as though it's a catalog capable of being recovered in case of disaster. VSAM increases your chances of recovery by maintaining two copies of critical file allocation data. The extra copy is stored in the *catalog recovery area* (also known as CRA).

By using the duplicate information stored in the CRA, these special AMS commands may enable you to recover a damaged catalog. In other words, it might be possible to replace the damaged information with the good copy. These commands are:

LISTCRA   The LISTCRA command compares catalog data with the corresponding CRA entry. Any differences are flagged to draw attention to potential catalog errors.

EXPORTRA   The EXPORTRA command is similar to EXPORT. Using CRAs, it can reference objects not addressable by the damaged catalog. EXPORTRA can be used to access these objects and create copies of them which can be moved back into the system via the IMPORTRA command.

IMPORTRA   The IMPORTRA command is similar to IMPORT. This command is used to reestablish in a catalog any objects which have been copied with the EXPORTRA command. Using information con tained on the exported file, IMPORTRA reconstructs the related catalog entries.

RESETCAT   The RESETCAT command copies CRA infor- mation back to the catalog. The two DASD volumes are compared and any mismatched information in the catalog is replaced with that from the CRA.

SECURITY

Security is a subject that should open up several topics for discussion in a well-organized data center. One aspect of security is adequate file and catalog recovery procedures. That's where such AMS commands as EXPORT, IMPORT, LISTCRA, EXPORTRA, IMPORTRA and RESETCAT come into play.

Another security consideration is the distinction between test and production files. Can you imagine what a fiasco would occur if test files got mixed up with production files, especially if the Payroll System suddenly doubled everyone's salary? Insuring that such a situation doesn't occur is part of a good security plan.

Most data centers develop distinctions for test and production files. It's a sensible idea I strongly recommend. How- ever, don't be misled into believing that naming conventions alone secures files.

PASSWORD PROTECTION

VSAM allows you to password protect files. This security feature helps protect data from unauthorized usage. Basically, an application program cannot process a secured file unless the computer operator supplies VSAM with an authorized password.

How do you password protect files?

Optional parameters available with the DEFINE command allow you to create password protected files. If you omit all such parameters, the file remains unsecured and no password is required for access purposes. Different levels of security may even be specified with each level requiring a separate password. These levels and their associated AMS parameters are:

Level	AMS Parameter
Full access	MASTERPW
Control access	CONTROLPW
Updata access	UPDATEPW
Read access	READPW

Full access—User may perform any I/O operation on the secured object. If the object is a catalog record, a valid MASTERPW will allow you to delete an entire file and to alter password requirements or any other information in the catalog pertinent to a file, index or catalog.

Control access—User may retrieve and store the contents of a CI rather than an individual record. Data contained in the CI may be read and changed.

Update access—User may retrieve, update, insert and delete records in a file. If update access is specified for a catalog, files may be defined in it.

Read access—User may read records only. Modifications to a file are not allowed. If read access is specified for a catalog, password information will not be listed when the LISTCAT command is executed.

The four levels of passwords supported by VSAM can be organized in a hierarchy:

READPW
UPDATEPW
CONTROLPW
MASTERPW

This list is organized from the lowest to the highest passwords. Each higher-level password allows all operations permitted by lower levels. For example, if UPDATEPW is specified, all operations associated with the READPW are also allowed. If a password other than the MASTERPW is specified, it's typically referred to as a low-level password. If a low-level password is specified, then a master password must also exist. Does that mean you have to code a MASTERPW? Not necessarily. The AMS DEFINE and ALTER commands will propagate the value of the highest password specified to all higher password levels. For example, if an update password (UPDATEPW) is the only password coded, it automatically becomes the control access and full access passwords also.

How do you supply a password?

There are a couple of ways to communicate the password if the object has been secured. If an AMS command is issued, follow the file name with a slash and then the password:

DELETE INV.MASTER.FILE/INVZ32Z1

Here, the password for INV.MASTER.FILE is INVZ32Z1.

Batch programs referencing password protected files may logically supply passwords. In an assembler program, the ACB macro for the VSAM file may contain the password, and COBOL supports a PASSWORD clause for a file's SELECT statement. Both require that the program internally supply the appropriate password. This means that every time the password changes, so must these programs.

If you plan on changing passwords very frequently, you may want to explore the following option.

VSAM can prompt the console operator for the password. This process automatically occurs if the batch program doesn't logically supply the password. Note that I use the term "batch". For an on-line program, this prompting facility is not supported.

When the operator is expected to supply the password, you may wish to specify two additional parameters supported by the DEFINE command.

ATTEMPTS   Specifies how many times the console operator can attempt to enter the correct password before the program is aborted. A value of 0 through 7 may be specified. If 0 is coded, no attempts are allowed.

CODE   Specifies a name other than the file-ID of the data set to which the operator needs to respond with a password. The code name for a file may consist of one to eight characters. If you don't want the operator to know which password applies to which file, use this parameter. Code names rather than actual file-IDs are associated with passwords.

Another parameter associated with password security is AUTHORIZATION. This allows you to use a user security verification routine (USVR) along with VSAM's regular security facilities. If this parameter is specified, once a valid password is entered (other than a master password), then control is passed to the USVR where further checking may be performed to ensure that only authorized personnel are referencing the file.

11
CHAPTER

Recognize the Need for Standards

No matter what you do in DP, proper standards can mean success or failure for your job. Recognizing a need for standards is your first step towards being part of an organized, productive data center. Regardless of your job function, you have responsibilities, and it's important that you carry out those responsibilities in an efficient manner understood by others in the organization.

Why is it so important that other people understand how you perform tasks?

Perhaps you go on vacation and a coworker has to fill in for you. Many people in the organization may have the same job duties as you. Imagine how chaotic it would be if everyone performed them differently! Also, you may be promoted to a higher position with someone else assuming your present job duties.

Consistency and efficiency are two benefits every data center should reap from the implementation of standards. I can't tell you every single policy to implement. Although all data centers share many common characteristics, each also has its own unique personality. You and your coworkers must decide what is best for a particular organization. My goal is to emphasize the importance of developing and abiding by standards. I *will* now give you a few suggestions in regards to VSAM, but these ideas in no way constitute *all* policies your data center may need.

211

USER vs. MASTER CATALOGS

Establish user catalogs which will then in turn point to the master catalog. Multiple user catalogs may be created.

Establish guidelines as to the contents of user catalogs. For example, it may be desirable to establish separate catalogs for batch and on-line activities. Production and test work may warrant separate catalogs.

User catalogs will provide you with better recovery procedures. By placing everything in the master catalog, you limit available backup measures.

NAMING CONVENTIONS

VSAM files, like all other files, should follow naming conventions. I recommend prefixing each file with a three-position system ID. For example:

INV.MASTER.FILE
INV.TRANS
INV.LOG.FILE

Each of these files are part of the Inventory System; the INV prefix signifies this.

TEST FILES

It should be easy to distinguish test files from production files. You can accomplish this by loading them to separate user catalogs and placing a special identifier on the file-ID. Examples of the latter are:

INVT.MASTER.FILE

and

TEST.INV.MASTER.FILE

So, use a distinguishing characteristic and communicate it to everyone involved.

MONITORING

Monitor VSAM clusters on a regular basis. Use the LISTCAT command discussed in Chapter 9. Perhaps the best approach for your organization is to assign this responsibility to the programmer most familiar with the application.

CODING GUIDELINES

Develop coding guidelines pertinent to VSAM logic statements. Require FILE STATUS checking as opposed to INVALID KEY logic. Naming conventions may be instituted for status fields as well as record key fields:

```
01   FILE-STATUS-INV-MASTER              PIC XX.

     05   REC-KEY-INV-MASTER.
     10   INV-MASTER-CO                   PIC 99.
     10   INV-MASTER-ITEM-NBR             PIC 9(6).
```

RECOVERY

Always ensure that adequate backups are available. Catalogs as well as files need to have recovery provisions. For most applications, it's desirable to keep more than one generation.

Backups are often kept off-site as part of a disaster recovery plan. Consider which generations should be maintained in a secure place.

SECURITY

Standards regarding the creation and support of passwords should be developed. All or just some clusters may be secured with passwords. Determine if there is a real need for such security provisions before implementing them. Establish the criteria that constitute a need for password protection.

HANDLING ERRORS

The FILE STATUS code allows you to logically verify the success of all I/O operations. If problems are detected, it may be beneficial to print an appropriate message and then call a subprogram for abnormal job termination.

So, force the program to abend if I/O problems are detected.

A dump provides helpful information about the fields and files involved. Also, a dump is more noticeable than just a console or SYSLST message. It's too easy for these messages to go undetected and thus unreported.

For display messages I recommend exhibiting the:

1) Program name.
2) FILE STATUS code.
3) File identifier.
4) Type of I/O operation being performed.

Abends can be created by calling subprograms that force program dumps, or by calling subprograms that don't exist. The latter will show up as an EXTRN during the cataloging process. When a CALL statement is issued for it, an "operations exception" should occur, thus forcing a dump.

12

VSAM
Space Management

One of the great advantages of VSAM over ISAM is its disk management capability. If you've ever coded JCL statements to support ISAM files, you probably had a minimum of three EXTENT statements for each file—one for primary data, one for indexed keys, and one for overflow. Physical DASD space had to be allocated for each of these areas. Each time allocations had to be changed, all related EXTENT statements had to be changed.

VSAM, on the other hand, eliminates the need for EXTENT statements. Physical space allocations are accomplished through such AMS commands as DEFINE SPACE. Individual files no longer require separate track and cylinder allocations. A specific amount of DASD space can be allocated to a user catalog to be used by numerous clusters.

Let's say 12,000 tracks are allocated to INV.USER. CATALOG. Five clusters reside in this area. However, specific allocations are not needed for each of these five files. VSAM's disk management feature enables each file in a cluster to automatically acquire needed DASD space. Continuing with the INV.USER.CATALOG example, automatic allocations may be made as follow:

	TRACKS
INV.MASTER	5,320

DOS VSAM for Application Programmers

INV.LOG.FILE   230
INV.TRANS.FILE   572
INV.VENDORS   1,011
INV.ACCT.EXT   130

                    7,263

Note that only 7,263 of the 12,000 tracks are used. In other words, we have room for growth. Such growth can take the form of expansions to existing files or even the addition of new files. In either event, disk management occurs without our assistance. Space is found in the allocated area for a file and is then used. When the file is physically deleted with the AMS DELETE command, VSAM will reallocate the same space to other data sets.

Of course, files can grow beyond the capacity of the cluster's allocated space. You may then be faced with expanding cluster size; however, that's quite a bit easier than having to fool with numerous EXTENT statements!

VSAM isn't the only access method that can benefit from this function; SAM files can also be automatically managed. The VSAM Space Management for SAM feature is specifically geared towards DASD management for your SAM files. VSAM users who are already comfortable with the AMS program often find it desirable to have their sequential files afforded the same advantages. Briefly, these are:

1) Reduces the planning, organizing and maintenance efforts needed to allocate DASD space.

2) Eliminates the need to consider the physical location of files, DASD characteristics, block sizes and blocking factors.

3) Allows you to define and process SAM files within VSAM data space.

4) Affords file security protection through the use of passwords.

5) Provides AMS commands for performing such utility functions as PRINT, REPRO, etc.

6) Affords file-monitoring capabilities when the LISTCAT command is used.

216

Sequential files managed under this facility are referred to as a SAM ESDS structure. They are *not* the same as VSAM ESDSs.

When you're looking at converting SAM files to this facility, some restrictions as to file characteristics apply. For example, spanned records are not supported; COBOL programs with a RECORDING MODE S clause will not function properly. Another restriction is that user labels are not supported. In the vast majority of cases, though, you should be able to convert your programs without any problems.

If you're interested in using the Space Management for SAM facility, consult the IBM reference manuals listed in the Bibliography; Using the *VSE/VSAM Space Management for SAM Feature* (SC24-5192) is an excellent text to begin with.

A
APPENDIX

File Status
Error Codes

A FILE STATUS error code with a value of 24 or more is usually indicative of a serious error condition that cannot be handled through program logic. The recommended action for these codes is program termination.

Each data center should develop standards as to what action should be taken when error codes exist. Policy examples are calling subroutines to obtain program dumps when certain values occur, stopping the console to display warning messages, etc.

FILE STATUS	PROBABLE CAUSE
00	Successful completion of I/O action.
02	Duplicate key encountered and DUPLICATES specified in the File Select statement. Successful completion of I/O action.
10	End-of-file has been encountered.
21	Sequential access only. Record is out of sequence.
22	Duplicate key encountered. DUPLICATES has not been specified in the File Select statement.
23	Direct access only. Requested record not found.
24	KSDS or RRDS only. No more space allocated to file.

FILE STATUS	PROBABLE CAUSE
30	Uncorrectable I/O error. May be caused by a data check, parity check or transmission error.
34	ESDS only. Request was issued to write a record beyond its externally-defined boundaries.
90	Unusable file—possibly an empty file opened as I/O. VSAM logic error.
91	Password failure.
92	Program logic error. Issuing an I/O statement for a file which has not been opened will result in this error. Other examples are: OPEN File is already opened. CLOSE File has not been opened. START File not opened. READ End-of-file has already been reached. WRITE Incorrect key for a file opened in the EXTEND mode. REWRITE No previous READ issued (sequential access). DELETE No previous READ issued (sequential access).
93	Insufficient virtual storage available.
94	No current record pointer for a sequential READ statement.
95	Conflicting file attributes. Examples are an attempt to open a KSDS as if it were an ESDS, record key length that does not match what was specified when the file was defined using IDCAMS, and file entries missing from catalog. Invalid or incomplete JCL statements may cause this error.
96	Missing DLBL card.
97	File not closed by previous job.

B
APPENDIX

VSAM
Organizational
Structures

KSDS	ESDS	RRDS
Records are physically organized by primary key.	Records are physically organized in the order in which they are entered.	Records are physically organized by relative-record number.
Sequential or direct access is supported. Direct access is by key or RBA.	Sequential or direct access is supported. Direct access is by RBA only unless you build an AI over the file.	Sequential or direct access is supported. Direct access is by relative-record number.
A record's RBA can change.	A record's RBA cannot change.	A record's relative-record number (slot number) cannot change.
May have one or more AIs.	May have one or more AIs.	May not have AIs.
Distributed free space is used to insert new records. Also used to change an existing record's length.	Space located at the end of the file is used for adding records. Record length cannot be changed.	Empty slots in the file are used for adding records. Record length cannot be changed.
Physical space given up by a deleted or shortened record is reused by new or lengthened records.	A record cannot be physically deleted.	Physical space given up by a deleted record can be reused by inserting a new record with the same relative-record number.

KSDS	ESDS	RRDS
Can have spanned records.	Can have spanned records.	Cannot have spanned records.
Can be reused as a work file unless it has an AI.	Can be reused as a work file unless it has an AI.	Can be reused as a work file.

Bibliography

The following IBM manuals were used as reference documents during the preparation of this book. If your data center is supporting VSAM files, I recommend that a copy of each manual listed be placed in your technical library.

Introduction to IBM Direct-Access Storage Devices and Organization Methods, GC20-1649

VSE/VSAM General Information, GC24-5143

DOS/VSE System Management Guide, GC33-5371

DOS/VSE System Control Statements, GC33-5376

DOS/VSE Access Methods Services—User's Guide, GC33-5382

DOS/VSE Entry User's Guide, GC33-6047

Using VSE/VSAM Commands and Macros, SC24-5144

VSE/VSAM Programmer's Reference, SC24-5145

VSE/VSAM Messages and Codes, SC24-5146

Using the VSE/VSAM Space Management for SAM Feature, SC24-5192

Index

DOS VSAM for Application Programmers

CATALOG, 103, 108, 116, 120, 122-125, 141, 202, 204
catalog recovery area (CRA), 206
catalogs, 12, 70, 129, 140
    coding requirements, 72
    hierarchy of control in, 78-80
    job, 77-78
    parameters for, 78
    recovery in, 196, 205-207
    relationships in, 73
catname, 116, 120, 123, 125, 202
CCHHR, 150
central processing unit, 2
CHAIN, 92
CHARACTER/HEX/DUMP, 129
CI/CA, 146, 189
CIFORMAT, 146
CISIZE, 146, 189
CKD devices, 154
class, 25, 45, 58, 149
CLOSE, 29, 32, 49, 51, 62, 63
CLUSTER, 97, 142, 145
clusters, 11, 43, 75, 109, 137, 141, 150, 151
    AMS utility, 84
    entry sequenced files, 44
    key sequenced files, 20, 117
    monitoring worksheet for, 192-195, 212
    relative-record files, 57, 117
    sequential vs. random processing, 189
    space allocation and, 191
COBOL
    entry sequenced files, 45-53
    key sequenced files, 24-29
    relative-record files, 57-69
COBOL compiler, 29, 48
code, 75, 151, 210, 213
command-set, 90
commands, AMS utility, 82, 83
comments, AMS utility, 85
comparand, 89
comparison test, 34
condition codes, AMS utility, 88, 89, 91
CONNECT, 205
control area (CA), 17, 22, 23
    entry sequenced files, 44
    record capacity of, 104
    size of, 191
    structure of, 17
control interval (CI), 13-14, 20-23, 29, 54, 56
    CA structure and, 17
    size of, 184
    structure of, 16
    valid size for, 14
control interval definition (CIDF), 17

control interval split, 24
control statements, AMS utility, 84
CONTROLINTERVALSIZE parameter, 112, 184
CONTROLPW, 151, 208
conventions, 211-214
COUNT, 131, 134
CREATION, 151
cross partition, 114, 115
cross system, 114, 115
cross-reference tables, entry sequenced files, 43
current record pointer, 30
CYLINDERS, 99, 102, 104, 107, 111, 120, 150
CYLS/VOL, 155

D

DASD, 1, 12, 16, 18, 96
    space management, 18
DATA, 142, 145
data buffers, 188
data centers, 118
data component, 11, 20, 21
data components, 11, 20-21, 109, 129, 141, 145, 146, 150, 151, 152, 191, 192
data division
    entry sequenced files, 48
    key sequenced files, 28-29
    relative-record files, 61-62
data name, 26, 27
data organization, VSAM, 11-18
DATA RECORDS clause, 29, 49, 62
data set, 7, 11, 18, 43, 71
    non-VSAM, 72
    placement of, 191
data space, 11, 71, 106, 137, 144
data space group, 149-150
data-name, 46, 58, 60, 63
DATASETS, 149
DATASETS-ON-VOL, 155
DATASPCS-ON-VOL, 155
default models, 118
DEFINE, 97-98, 138, 187, 198, 207, 209
DEFINE ALTERNATEINDEX, 86, 118-121
DEFINE CLUSTER, 86, 108-118, 188
DEFINE MASTERCATALOG, 86, 98-101
DEFINE PATH, 86, 121
DEFINE SPACE, 86, 101, 105-108
DEFINE USERCATALOG, 86, 101-105
DELETE, 29, 34, 39, 41, 49, 56, 62, 68, 69, 122-124, 138
DELETE ALTERNATEINDEX, 86
DELETE CLUSTER, 86
DELETE MASTERCATALOG, 87

224

Index

VOLUME output, 158
LISTCRA, 87, 206, 207
LOCK, 32, 51, 63
LOCK-BLOCK, 154
LOW-CCHH, 154
LOW-KEY, 154
LOW-RBA, 154
lowkey, 113

M

MARGINS, 93
master catalog, 71, 78, 79, 103, 116, 124, 196, 212
  non-VSAM data set, 72
MASTERCAT, 149
MASTERCATALOG, 97
MASTERPW, 100, 103, 151, 208, 209
MAX-EXT/ALLOC, 155
MAX-PHYREC-SZ, 155
MAXCC, 89, 90, 91
maximum condition code variable (see MAXCC)
MAXLRECL, 146
MAXRECS, 146
message code count, 94
message number, 94
messages, AMS utility, 93-94
  severity identifiers, 94
modal commands, 82, 88, 89
MODEL parameter, 109, 118
monitoring, 212

N

name, 25, 46, 58, 98, 101, 119, 121, 142
NAME parameter, 110, 111
naming conventions, 84, 212
NEWNAME, 125
NEXT, 37, 66
NOALLOC, 147
NOCIFORMAT, 147
NOERASE, 147
NOIMBED, 147
NOLABEL, 200, 203
NONINDEXED, 147
NONSPANNED, 147
NONUNIQUEKEY, 147
NONVSAM, 145
NOREPLICAT, 147
NOREUSE, 147
NOTUSABLE, 143, 147
NOUPDATE, 147
NOUPGRADE, 147
NOWRITECHK, 147
NULL, 151

null clause, 90
number, 89
NUMBERED, 113, 147

O

OBJECTS, 202
OFF, 92
offset, 113, 120
on-line processing, 2, 3, 18
OPEN, 29, 30, 49, 50, 62, 63
operating systems, 18
OPTIONAL clause, 45
ORDERED/UNORDERED, 113, 147, 190
ORGANIZATION clause, 25, 46, 58
OUTFILE, 127, 132, 200, 203
OVERFLOW, 154
overflow area, 5
OWNER-IDENT, 151

P

parameter set, AMS utility, 83
PARM, 88, 91, 93
partition dumps, 92
PASSWORD clause, 26, 30, 46, 50, 59-62, 209
  AMS utility, 86
passwords, 18, 58, 99, 100, 103, 108, 116, 119-127, 199, 200, 207-210
  hierarchy of, 208
  levels of, 208
PATH, 97, 145
PATHENTRY, 121
paths, 121, 145, 146, 150, 151
performance factors, 191-192
PERMANENT, 201
phase name, 82
PHYRECSA/TRK, 154
plus symbol, AMS utility, 85
portability, 18
positional parameter, AMS utility, 83
primary allocation, 99, 102, 107, 111, 119
PRIME, 154, 155
prime data area, 5
PRIMEDATADEVICE, 201, 204
PRINT, 87, 90, 127-132
  sample output from, 128
procedure division
  entry sequenced files, 49-53
  key sequenced files, 29-39
  relative-record files, 62-69
PROTECTION, 144
protection group, 151-152
PURGE/NOPURGE, 124, 151, 204

227

This book may be kept

FOURTEEN DAYS

A fine will be charged for each day the book is kept overtime.

GAYLORD 142

PRINTED IN U.S.A.